Penrith

A Historical Record in Photographs

A PENRITH MUSEUM ALBUM

Penrith - A Historical Record in Photographs

Copyright © Eden District Council.

ISBN 0-9538313-0-2

Text by Judith Clarke and Sydney Chapman, Penrith Museum.
Title page: photograph by Val Corbett.
Designed by Design & Business Services Graphic Design.
Printed in Great Britain.
Published by Eden District Council.

Contents

▲ **Two early photographic studies of Penrith.**

The view of Devonshire Street, above, by J Lomax, Artist and Photographer, may have been taken at the time of the town's celebrations for the marriage of the Prince of Wales with Princess Alexandra of Denmark on 10 March 1863; the words 'Prince of Wales', though faded, can be deciphered on the decorated arch. The photograph of Sandgate, below, was probably taken around the same date, though the photographer is not known.

Preface

The advent of photography in the late 1830s provided a new and exciting method of making visual records. Its capacity for accurately recording details far surpassed even the finest efforts made by artists using traditional materials. Louis Daguerre, appropriating the researches of Nicéphore Niépce, achieved wide public acclaim with the announcement in 1839 that he had 'fixed' a detailed image onto a silvered copper plate. However, each 'daguerreotype' was a unique object and could not be used to make more than one image. William Henry Fox Talbot's calotype process, which he discovered in 1840 and patented in 1841, was the direct ancestor of modern photography, for it involved the creation of both paper negative and positive images, making it possible to produce multiple prints. This method, with various modifications, was popular until the early 1850s, when it was superseded by the wet-collodion-on-glass process.

By the late 1850s the photographic revolution was well under way. Due to the expense involved, early photography was very much the preserve of the leisured and wealthier classes. Inevitably, this has biased the view of Victorian life portrayed in the photographic collections of present day museums, libraries and public archives. At least until the later nineteenth century, photographs tended to depict the lifestyles and interests of the upper and middle classes rather than the social life and work of ordinary men and women who, when they were featured, were introduced for quaint or curious effect. The introduction in 1888 of George Eastman's portable Kodak roll-film camera signalled the demise of such exclusivity and ushered in the era of the popular record or 'snapshot'.

The first recorded 'photographic artist' in Penrith was William Elliott of Crown Square, a local man who is first mentioned in KELLY'S POST OFFICE DIRECTORY of 1858. He continued in business for twenty-six years being last mentioned in BULMER'S DIRECTORY of 1884. Over time other 'photographic artists' appeared; SLATER'S DIRECTORY of 1896 records William Bolton of Castlegate Head and Thomas Ogle of 26 Arthur Street. The latter advertised in the PENRITH OBSERVER of that year, 'portraits of the late Rev W Brewis price 1s'. The work of these early photographers is rare and historically important. As one photographic business closed and another opened names such as James Huff, Abel McDonald, Edward McDonald, E Fowler Richards, and W J Usherwood are recorded. KELLY'S DIRECTORY of 1914 lists four photographic businesses; Albert Fallowfield, Charles Fearnsides, William Tunley, and Frederick & William Harrison who had taken over Edward McDonald's studio. In 1912 chemist J Cowper started advertising 'photographic materials' in the local press, testifying to the burgeoning hobby of the amateur which has never since lost its allure.

Crozier Lodge at the head of Sandgate by Thomas Ogle, c1865.

Built in 1826 by William Harrison, a Penrith gunsmith, the house was named after his wife, Ann Crozier. By the 1850s the Rev William Brewis had the tenancy and during this time Samuel Plimsoll, the 'Sailor's Friend', was an occasional visitor. The Misses Brewis ran a girls' school here until 1879.

A substantial number of prints, slides, glass plates and albums by many of these local photographers are preserved in the collections of Penrith Museum and biographical information about several of them appears in this book. Though most pursued their interest at a professional level, others, such as Colin Denwood, have used their skills as amateurs to provide documentary studies no less valuable or revealing. Colin, a local schoolmaster and founder member of the Penrith Photographic Society, recorded changes in the town throughout the 1960s and 70s and it is perhaps for his skills as a photographer that he will be best remembered. In these pages we encounter the work of contemporary photographer Freddie Wilson, who for over twenty years has recorded the events and people of the area for the CUMBERLAND AND WESTMORLAND HERALD and, in contrast, that of Barry Stacey and Val Corbett, which seeks to capture the essence and character of the local landscape.

One field of photography represented in the Museum's collection but which cannot, unfortunately, be dealt with in this book is cine film. Especially relevant is 'OUR TOWN', made in 1961 with the expertise of the BBC staff employed at Skelton - an early exercise in fly-on-the-wall documentary. It has rapidly acquired value as social history and reflects a time when a more leisurely pace of life was beginning to quicken. Steam trains that had shuttled townsfolk and tourists to and fro were still about, but in decline, and motorised road traffic was in the ascendant.

It is said 'the camera never lies'. However, while it has the potential to portray reality with an unrivalled directness, we cannot always take its results on trust. Those taking the photographs select, structure and in some sense shape what is recorded. It is through their eyes that we in turn focus on history. Moreover, although photographers have always been able to modify their pictures, recent developments in digital technology have greatly extended the possibilities and the 'enhanced' image is now commonplace. This poses increasing challenges for the historian, who more than ever will have to judge to what extent pictures have been altered. The only known instances in this book are identified in their captions.

This publication profiles the diversity of images held by the Museum. They have been selected for their social and historical interest, as well as their artisitic qualities. Recognising the penetrating insights which photography can give, Penrith Museum continues to collect images of the Eden area, historic and contemporary - a legacy through which future generations may in turn interpret their heritage.

▲ **Mrs Barbara Davidson of Penrith, c1885.**

This carte-de-visite by William Elliott has an advertisement on the reverse for his photographic business at 24 Crown Square which incorporates the royal coat of arms, almost certainly denoting an earlier commission to record a visit of a member of the royal family to the locality. Cartes-de-visite were stiff pieces of card about the size of a formal visiting card of the 1850s (hence the name). Patented in 1854 by A A Disderi and popularised by him in the following decades, they normally bore carefully posed studio portraits and were made by the millions worldwide, often for collection in family albums.

PENRITH CASTLE.
English Lakes,   No. 905.

▲ **Penrith Castle, c1868.**

This picturesque composition evokes the rural occupations and economy of the district; the huge tree-trunk can perhaps be seen as an allusion to the Forest of Inglewood which figured largely in the medieval records of the area.

Setting the Scene -
Penrith and District - Past to Present

The stones and slatt about Peroth looks so red that at my entrance into the town thought its buildings were all of brick, but after found it to be the coullour of the stone which I saw in the Quarrys look very red, their slatt is the same which cover their houses...

When Celia Fiennes the renowned traveller visited Penrith in 1698 she imagined it, judging from its reddish appearance, to be built of brick, though she soon realised it was of the same red stone she had seen in the quarries nearby. Formed some 260 million years ago when the area was part of an arid desert, the colour of the sandstone gives the town much of its distinctive appearance and character, and perhaps its name. PENRITH is thought by some to refer to the town's situation under the 'red hill'; others interpret it as meaning either 'head ford' or 'chief seat'.

FROM CELTIC CAPITAL TO MARKET TOWN

That Penrith is of great antiquity admits no doubt: this is sufficiently proved by the various unquestionably ancient monuments still in existence in its neighbourhood.

[WILLIAM HUTCHINSON, HISTORY & ANTIQUITIES OF CUMBERLAND, 1794]

Although the great monuments at Mayburgh, King Arthur's Round Table and Long Meg and Her Daughters indicate that the Penrith area has been inhabited by man since prehistoric time, little is known of the site of the future town through the Roman occupation and the 'Dark Ages'. The Roman military station 'Voreda', at Old Penrith, was situated beyond Plumpton, about six miles north of the present settlement, while to the south-east the strategically important fort at Brougham, called 'Brocavum', guarded the crossing over the River Eamont. After the Roman departure tribal identities gradually reasserted themselves over their pre-Roman territories.

Rheged was one such territory and appears to have included most of the north-westerly part of what the Romans described as Brigantia. It extended north into Galloway and its southern limits have been variously set at the Lune Gorge, the Ribble and the Mersey. Poems ascribed to the Celtic bard Taliesin record the exploits of the most celebrated king of Rheged, Urien, and his son Owain, who are said to have lived at Lywyfenedd, possibly the land around the river Lyvennet near Penrith.

Legend links Urien and Owain to Arthur and the Knights of the Round Table. The 'CYMRY' (fellow-countrymen) of Western Britain, that is to say of Strathclyde, Cumbria and Wales, were united in their opposition to invasion by the Saxons; the call to arms to expel the Saxon aggressors is at the core of the Arthurian legends. The wealth of stories and myths about Arthur and his followers and foes which are connected with North Cumbria and often commemorated in place names, is a reminder that it was here they were first shaped into heroic orally transmitted verse by bards of the Celtic community. Later, under pressure from Anglo-Saxon settlers, the cult of Arthur receded into local folk memory until it was revived in the Middle Ages. Arthur may well have been a historical figure, a sixth century British military leader, but it is as a mythical hero, an immortal warrior, that he has assumed particular importance. As the most popular and the most romantic of the Celtic heroes, our fascination with him shows no sign of diminishing.

The power of Rheged decreased after the death of Urien in the later sixth century, and in the seventh century it was absorbed by the expanding Anglian kingdom of Northumbria; for nearly three centuries the area was under Anglian influence. Extending southwards from Carlisle to Penrith, the wide tract of forest called Inglewood, or 'ENGLEWOOD', was later named after these Teutonic invaders, originally from the region of Angeln, or modern-day Schleswig-Holstein in Northern Germany.

The decline of Northumbria from the late eighth century eventually made way for the annexation of Cumbria by the British kingdom of Strathclyde, which had its stronghold at Dumbarton, near Glasgow. Although subject to the kings of Strathclyde and later of Scotland, Cumbria in the ninth and tenth centuries appears to have been ruled by its own line of British kings and some historians believe that Penrith was the capital of a semi-independent state. The River Eamont, just south of Penrith, was possibly the boundary between Strathclyde and Northumbria in 927 when Constantine king of the Scots and the Cumbrian king Owen came to pay homage to Athelstan of Wessex, perhaps at Dacre, following his invasion of Northumbria earlier that year.

The Giant's Grave, Penrith (1833).

Published engraving from the drawing by Thomas Allom.

As Strathclyde expanded, Scandinavians, predominantly Norse, moved in from the west - from Ireland, the Isle of Man and the Scottish Isles, an immigration which seems to have been a peaceful one. The area in the tenth century must have been something of a cultural melting pot and the fragmentary stone crosses and 'hog-back' tombstones known as the 'GIANT'S GRAVE' and the 'GIANT'S THUMB' in St Andrew's Churchyard in Penrith show an intriguing mixture of traditional Anglian, Celtic and Norse decorative motifs. Impressive memorials, they most probably mark the burial site of a succession of rulers, war-lords or chieftains. Tradition maintains the 'Giant's Grave' to be the resting place of King Owen of Cumbria, who reigned from AD 920 to 937, and perhaps, as W G Collingwood suggested, the church at Penrith of that time served as the 'royal chapel of the Cumbrian kings'.

The Giant's Grave, Churchyard, Penrith (1840).
From the drawing by Samuel Bough.

In 1018 the last Cumbrian king, Owen the Bald, allied himself to Malcolm II of Scotland and was killed in battle against the English. This allowed Malcolm to take over Cumbria, which remained part of Scotland until 1032. Thereafter it was in English hands until Malcolm III invaded the north-west and Penrith once more came under Scottish jurisdiction, - a situation which continued until some time after the Norman Conquest. The Normans were slow to bring the northern part of Cumbria under their control; Domesday Book shows that only the Kendal area and the southern fringes of the Lake District were in Norman hands by 1086. It is likely that the township of Penrith was taken into the hands of the English crown in 1092, when the Conqueror's son, William Rufus, captured Carlisle.

After the Conquest William Rufus and Henry I parcelled out most of the region into 'baronies' and planted it with settlers to ensure loyalty and establish Norman customs. Penrith remained outside this baronial framework for it was situated within the confines of the

Royal Forest of Inglewood. The Normans were avid lovers of hunting and reserved an extensive area of land which stretched from Carlisle towards the flanks of the Lake District for this sport. At its core was the ancient tract of woodland from which the forest took its name.

Inglewood was crown property protected by stringent Forest Laws and remained under active royal management throughout the medieval period. Inevitably it provided opportunities for poaching and lawbreaking and had its own outlaws skilled in archery; Adam Bell, Clym o' the Clough and William Cloudeslie, northern equivalents of Robin Hood. The fame of Adam Bell became a national one, such that he could be mentioned by Ben Johnson in THE ALCHEMIST and Shakespeare in MUCH ADO ABOUT NOTHING as a by-word for a first rate marksman when Benedick protests:

...hang me in a bottle like a cat, and shoot at me; and he that hits me, let him be clapped on the shoulder and called Adam.

The earliest surviving document in which the name of the town is recorded is dated 1167, under the 'pleas' of Alan de Nevill of the Forest of Inglewood when the Sheriff rendered an account for 10 shillings for 'Penred Regis' (King's Penrith). In 1223 the Crown granted the town the right to hold a market and a fair; an extract from the Pipe Rolls of Henry III takes the form of a letter of command to the Sheriff of Cumberland -

Know that we desire that a market be held in our manor of Penred on the Wednesday of every week. And that a fair be held in the same place yearly from the Eve of Pentecost to last until the Monday next after the Feast of the Holy Trinity...

The town remained a royal manor for another nineteen years after Henry's market grant, during which time the counties of Cumberland and Westmorland continued to be claimed by the Scots. In 1242 a compromise was brought about by Cardinal Otho, the Papal Ambassador, and the Scots relinquished their claim on receipt of '200 librates of land' comprising the manors of Penrith, Sowerby, Langwathby, Great Salkeld, Carleton and Scotby, known collectively as the 'Honour' of Penrith. The town was again recognised as a Scottish possession, albeit one which the Scottish king held as tenant-in-chief of the English crown. His tenure depended not only on the usual homage and loyalty expected of a feudal tenant, but also on the payment of 'ONE SOAR-HAWK YEARLY' to be delivered at the castle of Carlisle, still an English stronghold. This situation was to last until 1295, when Edward I seized back Penrith, with the other manors, and it was once more restored to the jurisdiction of the English crown. Edward's determination to impose English rule on Scotland was responsible for much hatred between the two nations.

By the mid thirteenth century Penrith was of sufficient importance to merit its own official seal. Made of brass, the seal bears the cross of St Andrew, patron saint of the parish church, and the inscription 'SIGILLUM COMMUNE VILLE DE PENRETH' - the Common Seal of the Town of Penrith. In the mid nineteenth century the seal (now on display in Penrith Museum) was found over twenty miles away to the north-east, buried in the churchyard at Brampton. It has been suggested that it was carried there by the Scots after one of their raids on Penrith.

The long-disputed border between England and Scotland continued to be the cause of much strife down the centuries. The conflict was not solved until the Union of the Crowns in 1603. The fourteenth century saw almost ceaseless hostilities along the border and, like other settlements near it, Penrith was pillaged and burned on more than one occasion. The present layout of the town may reflect those troubled times, with several open spaces into which cattle and goods could be brought for safety. Its narrow lanes and small courtyards with confined entrances would also have had similar advantages. Although the present Beacon dates only from 1719, centuries before that fires were lit here to warn of the approach of Scottish raiders.

The destructive violence of those early days has meant that little remains of medieval domestic architecture; most dwellings, being of wooden construction, would have been burned to the ground. Of necessity, defensive stone towers were built (sometimes called 'PELES' after the wooden constructions they replaced). They featured a vaulted windowless ground floor, two upper floors, and a flat roof from which missiles could be hurled at attackers. The late fourteenth century stone tower which forms the nucleus of the present day Hutton Hall in Friargate would have provided refuge both for its owners and some of their livestock.

In 1396 the manor of Penrith was granted to Ralph Neville, Lord of Raby and first Earl of Westmorland, who was probably responsible for building Penrith Castle. Some nineteenth century historians believed the castle owed its existence to William Strickland who owned land in Penrith and later became Bishop of Carlisle. In 1397 Strickland had been granted a licence to 'crenellate' a building in Penrith - possibly the Bishop's Tower, which stood at the western corner of the castle. However, a more recent view takes Hutton Hall to be a likelier candidate for this crenellation. Traditionally, Strickland has also been credited with improving Penrith's water supply by linking the River Petteril to the River Eamont thereby improving the flow of water to Thacka Beck, which runs through the town.

Penrith Castle, April 13, 1775.
Engraving signed: I Pye.

Scottish raids were not the only source of anxiety for the people of Penrith, for the town suffered intermittent outbreaks of plague. The vicar of St Andrew's Church, William Walleis, recorded the great pestilence of 1597/98, prefacing the names of the dead in the parish registers with the words 'HERE BEGONNE THE PLAGUE (GOD PUNISMET) IN PENRITH'. So many people died that there was not enough room to bury them all in the churchyard and, once the nearby schoolyard was full of bodies, new graves were dug on the fellside. The disease continued to claim numerous lives until the winter of 1598, when Walleis wrote, 'HERE ENDED THE VISITATION', signifying the end of the epidemic. Reminders of this time are the Plague Stone outside Greengarth in Bridge Lane, and Plague Lonnin on the fellside between Beacon Edge and Croft Terrace where, according to an old belief, the birds never sing.

Penrith Castle (1822).

Published aquatint from the drawing by T H Fielding.

Despite these troubles, continuity of town administration allowed Penrith to develop and by the seventeenth century it had become a thriving and prosperous settlement. Edmund Sandford, Squire of Askham, in his account of Cumberland written about 1675, remarks on its flourishing markets and fairs:

In the head of the ancient forest of Inglewood, is seited the famous towne and honor of Penrith; a very fine towne, and great markett and merchants for all kindes of comodities: and a grand fair on Whitson Tuesday; and every fortnight till Lamas; for all things, horses and cattle, and wool and sheep, and ewes and lambs in especially.

XV

Over a century later James Clarke, in his SURVEY OF THE LAKES OF CUMBERLAND, WESTMORLAND AND LANCASHIRE of 1787, described its continuing prosperity:

Penrith has an excellent market on Tuesday, and a small one on Saturday...The markets here are disposed in a manner truly astonishing in so small a town: the wheat-market is in one part of the town; rye and potatoes in another; barley in another; oats and pease in another; live-cattle, horses, and hogs have also their distinct markets.

Most of these are marked on one of the maps he included in the book.

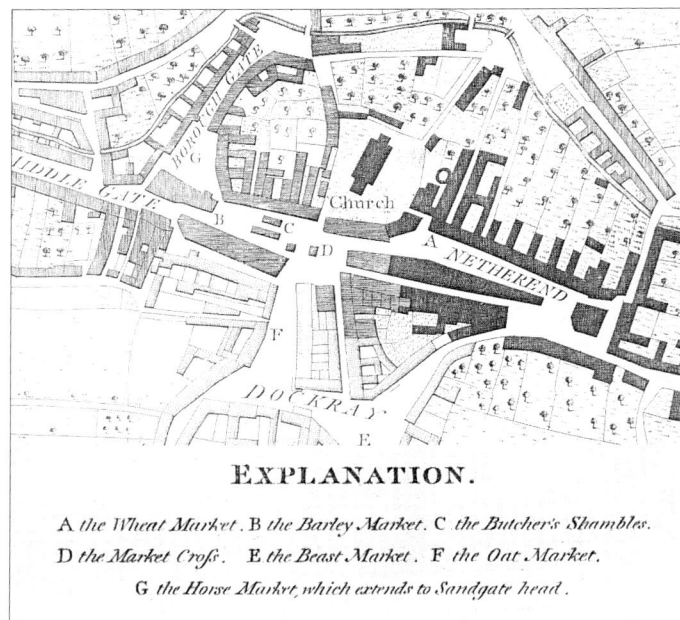

EXPLANATION.

A *the Wheat Market*. B *the Barley Market*. C *the Butcher's Shambles*.
D *the Market Cross*. E *the Beast Market*. F *the Oat Market*.
G *the Horse Market, which extends to Sandgate head*.

The letters 'C' and 'D' indicate the position of the butchers' shambles and the market cross in what is now Market Square and Devonshire Street, where there was also a Moot Hall and another building known as The Roundabout. By 1826 these had all been cleared away on the instigation of a Town Improvement Committee opposed to the cluttering up of the town centre with buildings.

Though primarily a market town, Penrith had some manufacturing industries too; dyeworks and weaving shops were recorded as early as 1310. In his 1787 SURVEY, Clarke noted that:

...there are some very considerable manufactories of checks, which are daily increasing; two common breweries in good employ; two hair-merchants, who (limited as their business may seem) are both men of property; and a tannery, where some business is done.

PENRITH TAN WORKS.

ROBERT CLARK,
Skinner, Tanner, Currier & Woolstapler.

Union Court, Penrith 185

Bot. of Robert Clark
Skinner, Tanner, Currier.
AND
WHOLESALE LEATHER DEALER.

Robert Clark's works, later Glasson's Brewery, Roper Street, Penrith.

Penrith was also an important clockmaking centre throughout the eighteenth century. The families of Cheesbrough and Porthouse were two of the pre-eminent makers in the county.

A younger contemporary of Clarke, also with close Penrith links, rose to the height of literary fame in the course of his long life - William Wordsworth. It was here and in the neighbourhood of the town that the story of his family in Cumbria began and where some of the major events in the poet's life were enacted; where his grandparents and parents were born and married, and where he was by his mother's side during her last days before she died and was laid to rest in St Andrew's churchyard. In the town he went to school with his sister Dorothy and the girl Mary Hutchinson who would one day be his wife. On Penrith Beacon he experienced the first of several 'SPOTS OF TIME', episodes formative of his poetry and character and there, later, felt a 'SPIRIT OF PLEASURE AND YOUTH'S GOLDEN GLEAM'. Unsettled and unhappy for a while when orphaned and living with his mother's family the Cooksons, in later years these difficulties were transcended and the region's history, centred around the plain of Eden, assumed greater significance for him. His earlier radicalism subsided and he became increasingly interested in tradition and continuity when the country as a whole was facing the inevitability of social change. He enjoyed the patronage of the Earl of Lonsdale which brought him into contact with other talented and influential local people such as the Quaker abolitionist, poet and guidebook writer Thomas Wilkinson who lived at Yanwath, and the Penrith-born artist Jacob Thompson.

The Wordsworth family played its part in local affairs. At the time of the 1745 Jacobite Uprising, the rebels accompanying the 'Young Pretender' Prince Charles Stuart on his retreat to Scotland were involved in hostilities which included a skirmish at Clifton just south of Penrith. Richard Wordsworth, who was then Receiver General, left his house at Sockbridge, two and a half miles from the town, seeking refuge in Patterdale with the County's money. His wife was left to guard the house and there she courageously entertained a party of Jacobite officers until Sir James Lowther and others ejected them from the area. Only months earlier the Prince had rested overnight in The George Hotel on his confident march south. A previous generation of Penrithians had experienced similar anxieties when in 1715 the supporters of the 'Old Pretender' were the cause of the beacon on the fellside above the town being fired in earnest to alert the district to the danger. A motley 'army' of yeomen and labourers carrying scythes and guns lost its nerve when faced with the rebel forces drawn up in battle order on Penrith Fell. They made off, leaving their commanders Viscount Lonsdale and Bishop Nicolson of Carlisle protected only by their servants and with no option but to flee.

Penrith's strategic position at the junction of the great mail and coach roads linking England and Scotland had also been highlighted by James Clarke, a land surveyor resident in Penrith whose acquisition of the Griffin Inn, Cornmarket, and the White Swan in Market Place in 1783 brought him into close contact with tourists:

Penrith is perhaps the greatest thoroughfare in the North of England: all the Irish now cross the sea at Port-Patrick, and consequently take this in their road to the Metropolis. Should they come by Whitehaven this is still their road: besides, since the improvements of the roads, those who are travelling from Scotland to London generally chuse this road...Those, likewise, whom a taste for natural beauties impells to visit the Lakes, always consider Penrith as a kind of home in these solitary regions; and the consequence is natural, all the inns here seem to vie with each other in attention, and strain every sinew in making the country as agreeable as possible.

Penrith from Arthur Street (c1830)
Published lithograph from the drawing by C Greenwood.

The coming of the railways further promoted the growth of tourism and increased the number of visitors arriving in Penrith en route for the Lake District. Rail links first came to the town when the line from Lancaster to Carlisle opened in 1846, followed by the Eden Valley Railway in 1862 and the Cockermouth, Keswick and Penrith Railway in 1865. The railway brought many benefits, especially in the carriage of goods and the export of farm produce.

Castletown Penrith. Railway Bridge. from an old Print.

In 1848 an outbreak of cholera in the county alerted some of Penrith's inhabitants to the town's insanitary state. Thacka Beck was still used as the main sewer while the slaughter of cattle, sheep and pigs in The Shambles, in the middle of town, left the streets in a disgusting state. Fevers were common and the death rate excessive. Despite much local opposition the Penrith Local Board of Health was set up in 1851 and a scheme was adopted to abstract water directly from the River Eamont. New waterworks were opened in 1854 and measures were also taken to raise the standard of the town's lodging houses, to improve the streetlighting, and to end burials in the over-crowded St Andrew's Churchyard.

The late nineteenth century marked the start of an era of rapid development in the town's history, the result of personal initiative as well as the advent of modern local government - the Penrith Urban District Council in 1894. Local subscriptions financed the building of the Jubilee Cottage Hospital; townsfolk also raised money for the building of a drill and concert hall. The golf club, first formed in 1890, eventually took over the old race-course site to the north of the town. The Alhambra in Middlegate was opened in 1910 as a roller-skating rink, theatre and public hall - and later became the town's first cinema.

In these years of rapid progress the telephone was introduced and the Urban Council took measures to provide the town with electric lighting, applying to the Board of Trade for a provisional order. The Council also brought in a new and pure water supply from Hayeswater, improved the old sewers and provided new sewerage works at Whinfell. The creation of the Castle Park on land adjacent to Penrith Castle attracted some fierce opposition but the Urban Council eventually opened its splendid new recreation grounds in 1923. Another large area for recreation was formed in 1928 when Kilgour's Field was purchased as a football pitch, followed in the 1930s by the addition of the adjoining Foundry Field. The 1920s also saw the building of the first council houses, mainly on an area of land called Scumscaw, now Wetheriggs estate. This continued after the war with the construction of many more, especially in the Flatt field to the north of Folly Lane, now Scaws housing estate, and at Pategill.

The town provided support and refuge through the crises of two world wars. During the First World War an Auxiliary Military Hospital was set up in St Andrew's Parish Rooms, Wordsworth Street Hall and at Skiddaw Grove. On the outbreak of the Second World War pupils and teachers from the Royal Grammar School in Newcastle-upon-Tyne were evacuated to Penrith, and the boys' bright blue blazers and caps became a familiar sight around the town. They shared school buildings with local children, the senior part of the school using the classrooms at Penrith Grammar School in the afternoons.

The evacuation was an episode which, ironically, enriched the cultural history of Penrith as it resulted in several talented individuals taking up residence in the town, writing and sharing ideas. These included Royal Grammar School teacher, poet and literary editor Michael Roberts, his wife the writer and editor Janet Adam Smith, and before her move to Matterdale Vicarage the scholar-poet Kathleen Raine. Evacuee Brian Redhead, later a notable writer, television interviewer and presenter of Radio Four's 'Today' programme, wrote movingly of his years at Penrith. Other young evacuees from Newcastle resided not far away at Cockley Moor, the home of Helen Sutherland; her house became a haven for artists such as Ben Nicholson, Winifred Nicholson and David Jones.

The photographic record which reflects this history demonstrates just how much has survived in Penrith unchanged over the centuries. The layout of the town centre is still largely medieval in pattern; a few late medieval and Tudor buildings remain, though much modified. The comparative peace after the Union of the English and Scottish Crowns in 1603 led to a period of rebuilding in the seventeenth, eighteenth and nineteenth centuries. In consequence many of the buildings date from these times. The predominant style in the central area is Georgian with sash windows and raised red sandstone window-surrounds under blue-green Westmorland slate roofs. Concern for the preservation of buildings of historic interest such as these means that in the future the greatest changes are most likely to occur on the periphery. Whilst Penrith retains much of the essential charm and dignity of a historic market town, commercial developments on the outskirts and major new leisure and tourism initiatives nearby bring challenging stimuli for economic growth, and, hopefully, new subjects for coming generations of photographers, amateur and professional alike.

Market Town

▲ Market Tuesday in Devonshire Street and Market Square, c1900.

In 1696 William III granted the Honour of Penrith 'with all rights, members, and appurtances whatsoever' to his Dutch favourite William Bentinck, Duke of Portland. Almost one hundred years later it was sold to the Duke of Devonshire. In 1854 the Penrith Local Board of Health obtained from the Duke a ninety-nine year lease of the market and fair rights, then in 1878 purchased the market rights outright for the sum of £4,140. The control of the markets passed from the Local Board to the Penrith Urban District Council on its creation in 1894, and subsequently to Eden District Council in 1974.

▲ **Market Square, looking towards King Street, c1905.**

In the years before motor transport the country people came to town on market days with their horse-drawn traps and carts, to sell their wares and buy supplies. They would put up at an inn of their choice, leaving the vehicles in front with their shafts projecting into the street, the horses stabled behind, mostly with access through a narrow lane at the side. It is said that each inn had a market woman in charge of a market room, and any purchases made in town were sent by the tradesman's errand boy to the hostelry indicated, where for a small fee the market woman took charge of them.

▼ **Cornmarket, c1895.**

In Cornmarket it was traditional that on market days different grains were sold outside the various inns; rye in front of the Black Bull, wheat beside the Black Lion, oats between the Fish and the White Hart and barley at the Griffin. In the early days toll was collected in kind, but in 1880 the Local Board of Health introduced a monetary charge and the old toll-dishes were no longer needed. They are now on display in Penrith Museum. By the end of the nineteenth century, due to imports of cheap grain, only oats were being offered for sale. Soon the only visual links with the farming economy were the stalls of the portable implement manufacturers and agricultural merchants which still appeared on market days.

Cornmarket, Penrith.

▲ **Cornmarket, 1999.**

The partial pedestrianisation of this area of town and the construction of the 'Market Cross' in 1983 has provided an attractive market venue for stall-holders on Tuesdays. (Photograph by Val Corbett)

▲ **Market Tuesday in Great Dockray, c1960.**

Penrith photographer J L Topaz has captured the bustle of what was then Penrith's largest open market. In earlier times bull-baiting took place here when it was an offence, punishable by a fine, to sell bull meat unless the animal had been tied to the bull-ring and baited by mastiffs bred for the purpose as this was supposed to make the meat wholesome. In later years the practice continued as a 'sport'. In more recent times Great Dockray was, like Sandgate, a traditional venue for the twice-yearly hiring fairs, which took place at Whitsuntide and Martinmas.

▲ **Great Dockray, 1999.**

Val Corbett's view of Great Dockray shows the traditional street market which still takes place every Tuesday. On other days the open space is used as a car park.

▼ Market Arcade, c1912.

An archway off Devonshire Street marks the entrance to the Market Arcade, erected by the Local Board of Health in the 1860s. It led to a spacious Market Hall which accommodated stalls for fresh fruit and vegetables, eggs, buttter and other dairy produce, and live poultry. It was also the venue for a wide range of events such as concerts, lectures and election meetings.

▲ **Devonshire Arcade and Food Hall, 1999.**

The Market Arcade, here photographed by Val Corbett, was redeveloped in 1991. Penrith has many speciality shops which bring people from afar. The town centre has retained its individuality, an increasingly rare quality nowadays when shopping centres tend to be dominated by national chainstores.

▲ **The Egg and Butter Market in Sandgate, 1914.**

During the First World War the Market Hall was commandeered by the Westmorland and Cumberland Yeomanry and the egg and butter market was relocated to Sandgate.

▲ **Stallholder at Penrith's Saturday Market, Skirsgill, 1999.**

In recent years the Saturday market, held at the auction mart at Skirsgill, has become a popular market venue.
(Photograph by Val Corbett).

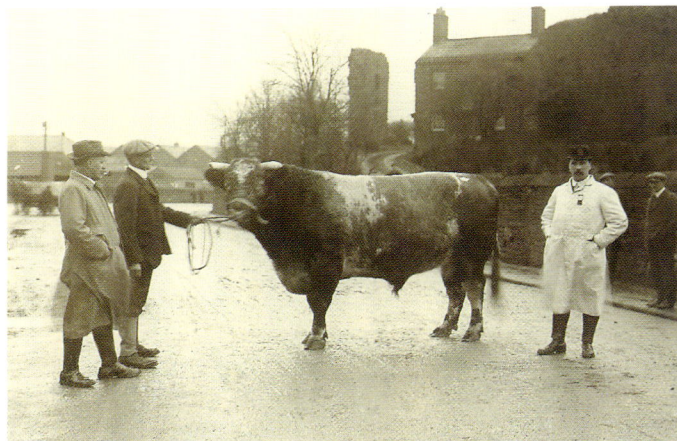

▲ **Cattle Fair, c1895.**

The cattle fair was on the Fair Hill, on the northern outskirts of the town above the White Ox Inn. William Furness in his HISTORY OF PENRITH published in 1894, tells us that in about 1832 'the Fair Hill was allotted to the Honor and Town of Penrith when the common was enclosed, as a place for holding fairs, and wherein the children of the town might play, the whole common having previously been their playground'.

▲ **Mr Tom Lowthian with his prize-winning bull, 1911.**

Prize-winning animals were often taken from the nearby auction mart to be photographed in front of the castle ruins. Penrith photographer Edward McDonald took this picture of Mr Lowthian of Winder Hall, on 10 January 1911.

▲ **Penrith Auction Mart, Skirsgill, 1999.**

An auction mart for the sale of cattle had been established in the town in the 1870s, called Penrith Farmers' Co. Ltd. Continuing as Penrith Farmers and Kidd's Auction Co Ltd, the mart was for many years situated near the railway station before moving to new premises at Skirsgill in August 1987. (Photograph by Val Corbett).

D2   Hidden Yards & Alleyways

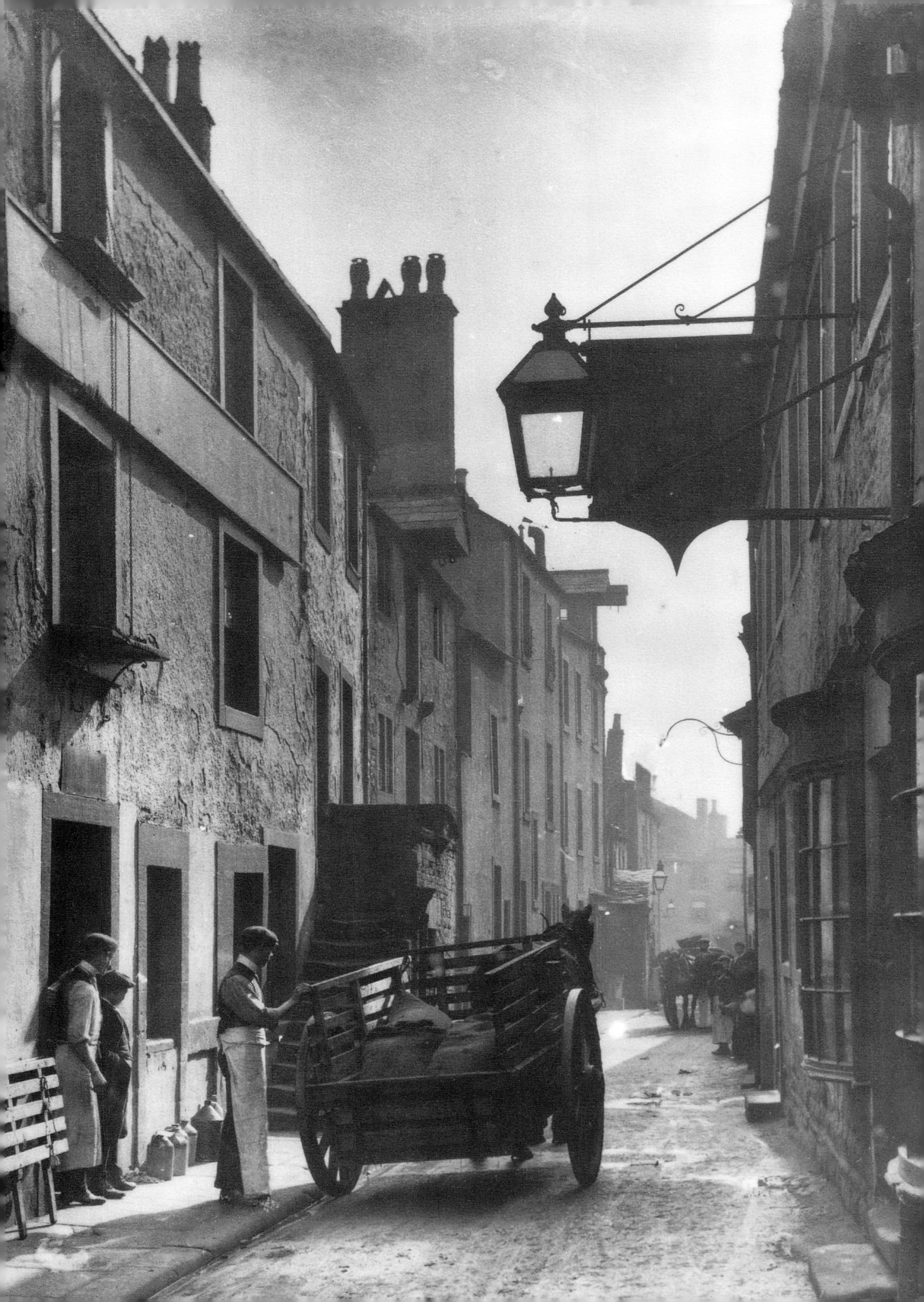

▲ Rowcliffe Lane looking north, c1900.

This photograph of Rowcliffe Lane presents a clear view of the two-storied premises which housed William Dean's pawnshop, and which in earlier days had been the manse attached to the Presbyterian church (now Princes Court apartments). A stone above one of the doors of the manse, dated 1656, is now in the wall of Reed's Printers premises in Southend Road. From the projecting upper floor window can be seen the elegant scrolled iron support from which William Dean's trade-sign used to hang. The photograph was probably taken shortly after 1897 when, according to KELLY'S DIRECTORY OF CUMBERLAND, William Henry Dean was still in business and living at 29 Wordsworth Street.

◄ Rowcliffe Lane looking south, c1900.

A scene at the turn of the last century looking down Rowcliffe Lane towards Crown Square shows Alcock's tea mart and grocery on the left. On the right are the premises of Guest's boot manufacture and repair shop which in earlier days had been the Black Lion Hotel, and before that the town's earliest post office. William Dean's pawnshop appears on the right. J E Horsley in his book JOTTINGS ABOUT OLD TIME PENRITH described the Lane as possessing 'some shops which it is probable have been used for commercial purposes for hundreds of years' though he dismissed the idea that the stage-coaches used it as a thoroughfare. The street was more popularly known as Old Post Office Lane.

▲ **Peartree Yard, c1895.**

Though the house in this photograph was knocked down in 1925, the yard is still there, standing between Southend Road and Victoria Road.

▶ **The entrance to Douglas Yard off Sandgate, c1900.**

The eighteenth century property adjoining Douglas Yard was eventually demolished. The cottages to the right in this photograph, which have been restored, were formerly part of Sandgate Hall, built by the Fletchers of Hutton in 1640. It was there in 1745 during the Jacobite Rebellion that the Duke of Richmond, after encountering the rebels at Clifton as they retreated northwards, lodged overnight as the guest of its owner Mr Grave.

▲ **St Andrew's Churchyard looking towards Market Square, c1950.**

The building in the centre of the photograph is dated 1709, though the predominant building style around the churchyard is Georgian. Many of the buildings feature smooth render, or 'stucco', and are colour-washed to mimic or contrast with the natural stone.

▲ **St Andrew's Place and the Tudor house, c1950.**

A building opposite the south-west corner of St Andrew's Church, commonly referred to as the 'Tudor' house, incorporates a survival of the earliest domestic architecture in Penrith. The projecting porch-like gable bears an inscription below the uppermost window 'RB 1563', recalling its owner, who is believed to have been Roger Bartram. Here, in later times, according to local tradition was the school run by Dame Birkett. Among its pupils in 1776 you would have found the future poet William Wordsworth and his sister Dorothy and the girl who would eventually be his wife, Mary Hutchinson, daughter of a Penrith tobacconist. The poet's forebears and relatives were more closely connected with the town and its surrounding district than is generally appreciated.

▶ **Angel Lane, 1999.**

The Lane probably took its name from the Angel Inn which stood at the Dockray end on the north side. It was gone by 1906 though the actual building, much altered, still stands. In 1811 the Lane was known as Silver Street. About half-way down, to the right in this photograph by Val Corbett, stood the Waggon and Horses Inn which by 1880 had been replaced by a temperance hostelry, the Exchange, in turn replaced by Howes drapery shop. The property was knocked down when Angel Square was developed and now the Bluebell Bookshop stands on the site. The name of the entrance to the Square, Exchange Lane, recalls the building's earlier history.

▶ **White Hart Yard, 1999.**

Through an archway leading off Cornmarket is the lane called after the old White Hart Inn which was mentioned as early as 1720, and from the beginning of the nineteenth century was a noted coaching inn. By 1920 it had ceased to be an inn and in 1922 Mr William Kerr, a well-known nurseryman, bought the property. He gave the facade a complete facelift though the upper floors, where the Penrith Players had staged their first productions, remained. On the other side of the entrance to White Hart Lane was the Griffin Inn, which was demolished in the early 1890s. The landlord here, until his death in 1888, was the retired wrestling champion William Jameson whose large collection of trophies can be seen at Penrith Museum.
(Photograph by Val Corbett).

ISM
1669

▷3 Historic Settlement

► **The Giant's Grave, c1900.**

The 'Grave' is a collection of two badly
weathered cross shafts and four Norse
'hogback' tombstones, all of tenth
century date, possibly marking the
burial place of Owen, King of Cumbria
from AD 920 to 937. There is some
confusion of stories and names regard-
ing the Giant's Grave for some accounts
link it to Owain son of Urien of the
Kingdom of Rheged in the sixth century,
and to the Arthurian legends. It has
also been seen as the burial place of
the mythical giant Sir Owen Caesarius,
sometimes called Sir Hugh or Sir Ewan,
who was supposed to have dwelt at
Isis Parlis, or the Giant's Cave, on the
banks of the river Eamont near
Penrith. The Grave was reputably
opened in the sixteenth century to
reveal 'the great Long Shank bones and
other bones of a man, and a broad
Sword besides'. The constant repetition
and mingling of fact with legend
around the Giant's Grave underlines
the long-standing significance of this
ancient site. Daniel Defoe visited the
Grave in 1724, and Sir Walter Scott in
1831, although he had seen it 'dozens
of times before'. More recently the
monument's mythical and heroic associations were recycled in an intriguing
fashion - a photograph of it received by
James Joyce from his patron Harriet
Weaver in 1926 inspired the opening
passage of FINNEGAN'S WAKE.

St. Andrews Church, Penrith.   RELIABLE

▲ **St Andrew's Church, c1900.**

Penrith Church was probably already an ancient religious site when it was given to the Bishop of Carlisle on the creation of the diocese in 1133. The church, which was rebuilt in 1720-22, incorporates a medieval west tower, and has been described as 'the stateliest church of its time in the county'. Though the architect is not known, there are strong similarities with the work of Nicholas Hawksmoor. Two brass chandeliers which hang in the nave were the gift of the Duke of Portland to the people of Penrith for their loyalty during the Jacobite uprising of 1745. Mural paintings in the chancel arch are by the Penrith-born artist Jacob Thompson.

▲ **Penrith Castle, c1900.**

Penrith Castle is situated on high ground overlooking the town, close to the railway station. Early historians attributed its construction to Ralph Neville, Earl of Westmorland and Lord of the Manor of Penrith from 1396 to 1425; the later theory that William Strickland developed the original fortress is now questioned by some authorities. In 1471 the castle was granted to Richard Duke of Gloucester who used it as his base during his period as Lord Warden of the Western Marches. By the mid 1500s it was in a state of decay, much of the stone having been removed for other buildings in the town. In the 1840s the castle was sold to the Lancaster and Carlisle Railway, later incorporated into the London and North Western Railway, and they had stables for their horses inside the ruins. By the turn of the century nurserymen Joseph Tremble and Sons had their market gardens behind the castle.

▲ **Penrith Castle Park, 1999.**

In 1919 the Penrith Urban District Council acquired possession of the castle and grounds. While the castle ruins passed into state guardianship, the grounds were retained by the Council and the Castle Park was opened on 24 May 1923. Though the opening was a day of merry-making and celebrations, the park project had been a controversial one with the Council divided on the expenditure, and townsfolk worried about how much would be added to their annual rates bills. (Photograph by Val Corbett).

▲ **Penrith rooftops - looking towards Beacon Fell.**

▶ **St Andrew's Church tower and Penrith rooftops.**

▼ **St Andrew's Churchyard looking towards the Tudor House.**

(Photographs by Val Corbett).

▲ **Robinson's School, Middlegate, c1895.**

The Latin inscription above the doorway, translated, tells us that the school was provided 'From the Monies of William Robinson, Citizen of London in the Year 1670'. Penrith born William Robinson, a wealthy grocer and coffee merchant, made his fortune in London. In his will he left '£20 a year, for ever, to the churchwardens of the parish of Penrith, for the educating and bringing up of poor girls in a free school, in reading and sempstry, or such learning fit for that sex, being the poorer sort, whose parents should be unable to pay for their learning'. In later years the building became a National Infant School, administered by the Carlisle Diocesan Education Committee. It closed on 1 April 1971 when the staff and pupils transferred to the newly built Beaconside School on Scaws Estate. Robinson's School was then acquired by the local authority for the purpose of establishing the town's museum and tourist information centre.

▲ Penrith Beacon, c1905.

Crowning the summit of the tree-covered hill which rises above the town on its eastern side, Penrith's Beacon is one of the most recognisable landmarks of the area. Built in its present form in 1719, it stands on the site of earlier signal fires that alerted the townsfolk to attack from Scottish raiders. Though the Beacon was last seriously used during the Jacobite Rebellion of 1745, Sir Walter Scott on a visit to Cumberland in 1804 recorded it as flashing a message of warning during a Napoleonic invasion scare. From the summit, 937 feet above sea level, there are impressive views over the Eden plain, the Pennines, the Lake District fells, and on a clear day, across to the mountains of southern Scotland beyond the Solway Firth. Tree growth in recent years has, however, tended to restrict the prospect.

▲ **Beacon Hill from Penrith Castle, 1890.**

The red sandstone which gives the town its distinctive appearance can be seen to greatest extent in the solid terraces of Victorian housing which ascend the lower slopes of the Beacon. The Penrith Building Society which was established in 1850 acquired land for new streets and allotted plots, by ballot, to members. Thus in 1851 Arthur Street was laid out, next came Graham Street in 1853, Low Lowther Street in 1861, High Lowther Street and Wordsworth Street in 1865. Mr Joseph Birkett, accountant of Foxton House, Lowther Street, acted as secretary until its dissolution in 1878. In the centre of this photograph can be seen the tall chimney of Pattinson and Winter's old mill. The chimney was demolished in 1936 and the mill is now converted into flats and offices.

▲ Beacon Hill from Brunswick Road, July 1904.

Brunswick Road, formerly Scott Lane, which had been widened from Corney Square to Blue Bell Lane and re-named, was ceremoniously opened to mark Queen Victoria's Golden Jubilee in 1887.

T·S
1690

D4   Some Influential Families

▲ **The 5th Earl of Lonsdale and his cars in front of Lowther Castle, c1910.**

The original Lowther Castle, which was built in 1690 by Viscount Lowther, burned down in 1720. Though the architect and designer Robert Adam was engaged to draw up plans for a new mansion in the Neo-Classical style, long delays coinciding with shifting tastes in architecture resulted in the adoption of a new design in the Gothic style by Robert Smirke. The work was carried out between 1806 and 1811 for William Lowther, 1st Earl of Lonsdale. At Lowther Castle the Earl entertained artists, writers and politicians including Sir Humphrey Davey, Sir Walter Scott and William Wordsworth (whose father had been employed as an agent to the Earl's father) who praised the scenic attraction of the castle and its grounds in his verse and in his GUIDE to the Lake District. During the later Victorian and early Edwardian period the family was represented by perhaps the most flamboyant of the Lowthers, Hugh Cecil Lowther (1857-1944), 5th Earl of Lonsdale, known from his livery as the 'Yellow Earl'. He is pictured here with his fleet of motor cars. He owned at least fourteeen, mostly Napiers, and, fittingly, accepted the position of first President of the Automobile Association following its amalgamation with the Motor Union in 1911.

▲ **Hugh Cecil, 5th Earl of Lonsdale and his wife Grace, Countess of Lonsdale, 1909.**

The Earl was an enthusiastic participator in sports such as yachting, hunting and horse-racing, winning the St Leger in 1922. He was also a keen supporter of boxing (the Lonsdale Belts). A few years after his death in 1944 the castle was closed and a series of auction sales, intended to offset considerable death duties, saw its contents dispersed.

▲ The visit of Kaiser Wilhelm to Lowther Castle, 1895.

Through his sailing pursuits the Earl of Lonsdale developed a friendship with Queen Victoria's grandson the German Emperor, Kaiser Wilhelm II. The Kaiser stayed at Lowther as the Earl's guest on two occasions, in 1895 and in 1902. Commenting on the former, the local press described how 'this visit has created a marvellous amount of interest and it will be memorable for generations to come'. The visit was recorded by Penrith photographer E Fowler Richards, and in this photograph the Earl appears in the centre of the middle row with his guest on his right, cigar in hand and coat on arm. The Earl's wife, Grace, Countess of Lonsdale is seated in front of her husband. The outbreak of war terminated their friendship and saw the Earl energetically promoting the war effort against Germany. Following the peace, however, they exchanged Christmas greetings until the Kaiser's death in 1941.

▲ **Welcoming party for the arrival of the Kaiser at Penrith Station, 1895.**

This photograph showing members of Penrith's first Urban District Council was taken near the railway station on 14 August 1895 as they awaited the arrival of Kaiser Wilhelm II en route to Lowther Castle as the guest of Lord Lonsdale. On the left is the Clerk, Mr George Wainwright, with Councillors Thistlethwaite, Fleming, Sweeten, Fairer, Slack, Scott, Ingledew, Altham, Winter and Neville. Two members, Councillors Seatree and Glasson, were not present.

▲ **The Lowther Woodmen, c1910.**

By a grant dated 1337 from Edward III, Hugh, son of Sir Hugh de Lowther, was permitted to enclose two hundred acres of land at Lowther, allowing him to keep deer for meat and to grow timber, a tradition of family land management that has continued until present times. Lowther Park which contains the historic deer park comprises about six hundred acres and has been described as representing the largest formal, man-made element in the landscape of the Lake District. At present the Lowther Estates cover seventy-two thousand acres, five thousand acres of which are woodland and include the plantation on Beacon Fell above Penrith.

▼ **Caroline Cottage on Beacon Edge, Penrith, c1900.**

Built in 1818 at the former entrance to Beacon Fell in an architectural style which recalls the Gothic design of Lowther Castle, the Keeper's Lodge was named Caroline Cottage after the 1st Earl of Lonsdale's youngest daughter. J Allison in his Picturesque Pocket Companion, published in 1836, tells us that 'a room in this building has been appropriated by the noble proprietor for the use of the inhabitants of Penrith, as a Public tea and music-room.' Presently, access to Beacon Pike, courtesy of the Earl of Lonsdale, is by a gently sloping path further west along Beacon Edge road.

▲ **Eden Hall mansion and gardens from the west, c1910.**

Eden Hall was built in 1821, in Italianate style, by architect Sir Robert Smirke for Sir George and Lady Musgrave. It replaced an earlier stone structure dating from Jacobean times which had its own private chapel. The elaborate flower gardens on the west front were designed by Sir George himself.

▼ **Eden Hall, c1910.**

The Musgrave family, formerly of Musgrave and later of Harcla Castle in Westmorland, were one of the most ancient in the Eden area. Their lands at Edenhall came through the marriage of Thomas Musgrave to Joan, coheir of William Stapleton. Sir Richard Musgrave who died in 1409 is said to have killed the last boar in Westmorland and as though to confirm the story a pair of boar's tusks were found in his tomb when it was being restored in 1847. It is thought that one of the Musgraves of that earlier era may have brought back from the Crusades the famous cup of Syrian glass known as the 'Luck of Edenhall' and now one of the treasures of the Victoria and Albert Museum. Legend, on the other hand, has it that it was given by fairies to a butler who was fetching water for the household from the well nearby. The subject of verses by Longfellow and the German poet Uhland, it was said to safeguard the family so long as it remained intact and in their ownership, having being delivered with the warning -

'If e'er this cup should break or fall,
Farewell the luck of Eden Hall'

Several such lucks, usually vessels or containers, were once to be found in the area, and were held to preserve the fortunes of their owners providing they were kept in their homes intact. Their talismanic properties and associations with fairies are perhaps a folk memory of the days when the beliefs of the Norse and Celts of Cumbria were still maintained alongside the Christian faith which regarded them as superstitions.

Eden Hall, Penrith.

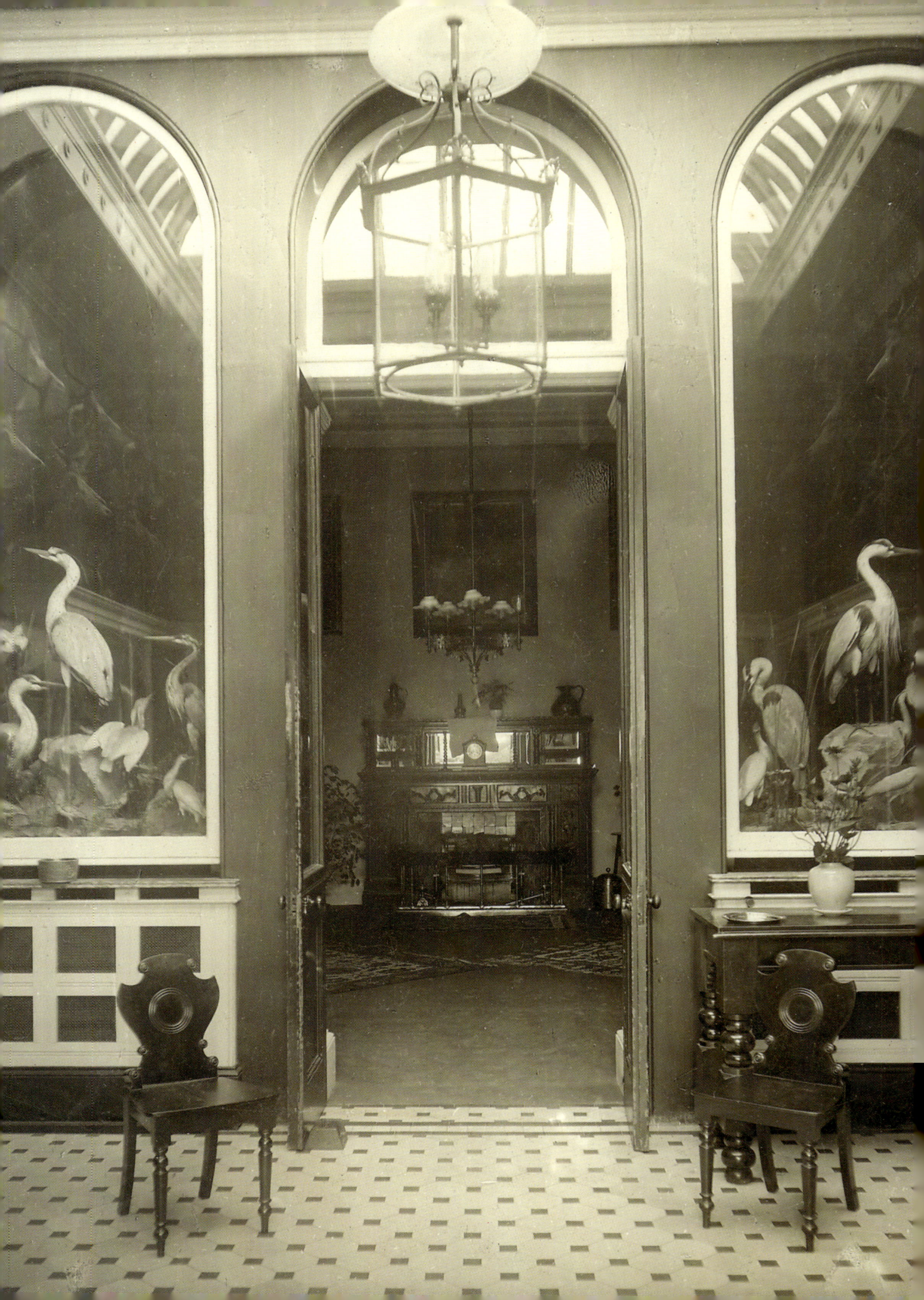

▲ Sir Richard George Musgrave of Eden Hall (1872-1926),

Sir Richard George's father, Sir Richard Courtenay Musgrave, had been elected a member of Parliament for East Cumberland in 1880, but after attending the Speaker's Dinner in February 1881 caught a cold waiting for his carriage and died soon after. His son and heir, Richard George, was only nine years old at the time. Later, his widowed mother, Adora alias Zoe, married Henry, 3rd Lord Brougham and Vaux, and left Eden Hall to join her husband at Brougham Hall. In 1894 William Furness dedicated his HISTORY OF PENRITH to Sir Richard George Musgrave, then aged twenty-two, and commented that 'he is a youth of great promise, and has already won the esteem and respect of his tenantry and the public, by his simple and unostentatious demeanour.' This photograph by E Fowler Richards was taken around this time. The family estates were later sold by Sir Richard, and Eden Hall was demolished in 1934 - ironically the year which also saw the destruction of Brougham Hall.

◄ The entrance hall, Eden Hall, c1910.

The elegant mansion contained many rooms, decorated with valuable antiques and family portraits. On either side of the inner doorway in the entrance hall were cases of stuffed birds. Collecting and displaying such material was a common feature of Victorian and Edwardian country houses. Some of the specimens in this photograph are now in the collections of Tullie House Museum at Carlisle.

▶ **The Musgrave Monument, Market Square, Penrith, c1890.**

Penrith still possesses a prominent reminder of the Musgraves and the high esteem in which they were held locally in the clock tower monument in the town centre. It was erected in 1861 as a memorial to Philip, the eldest son of Sir George and Lady Musgrave, who had died two years earlier in Madrid aged twenty-six. Penrith Museum preserves a number of artefacts given by the family or connected with them.

▲ **Musgrave Hall, c1900.**

Standing in Middlegate opposite Robinson's School, this was the home of a branch of the family of Penrith, Fairbank, and Plumpton descended from Thomas Musgrave and his wife Joan, daughter of William Stapleton of Edenhall. The arms of both families appear in the shield carved on the lintel. This branch failing in the male line in 1662, it passed by marriage to Lancelot Simpson who also acquired Fairbank. His son Hugh Simpson became Clerk of the Peace for Cumberland in 1710. By marriage to its coheir Elizabeth Pattenson, his younger son Thomas acquired the Carleton Hall estate. By the late nineteenth century it was the home of the Countess Ossalinsky. Owning land at Thirlmere, she was awarded substantial compensation for its loss in 1882 when the lake and surrounding lands were acquired for development as a reservoir by Manchester Corporation. Having rejected an initial offer of £20,000 the Countess took her case to arbitration and eventually agreed on the sum of £70,000. This was officially described as a 'liberal allowance' as indeed it would appear to have been since the annual rental derived from it had been only £500. In former times this corner of Middlegate was more peaceful; there being no northern exit, traffic followed a route by Fallowfield Bridge over Thacka Beck and along Queen Street. The building now houses the Penrith branch of the Royal British Legion.

▲ **The Armoury at Brougham Hall, c1905.**

Brougham Hall was purchased in 1726 by John Brougham of Scales in Cumberland from James Bird thereby restoring it to the Brougham family who had been linked with the village and manor of Brougham from early medieval times. The most famous representative of the family was Henry Brougham (1778-1868), 1st Baron Brougham and Vaux, and Lord Chancellor of England. Henry Brougham was a radical in politics and engaged in bitter local election campaigns against the Lowthers. He remodelled the building in the style of a feudal castle complete with baronial Armour Hall, pictured here by Penrith photographer Charles Fearnsides. The display of weaponry evokes the 'Age of Chivalry' and reflects the fascination with the Middle Ages which gathered momentum from the early years of the nineteenth century, and was epitomised in fiction by Sir Walter Scott. On account of its architecture, which is thought to draw upon elements of the designs for Windsor of Sir Robert Smirke (who executed the neo-Gothic Lowther Castle), and through later visits by the Prince of Wales in 1857 and again as Edward VII in 1905, Brougham Hall was sometimes spoken of as 'The Windsor of the North'. By 1934 the fortunes of the Brougham family had declined so much that the Hall was sold. It was substantially demolished but more recently has undergone extensive re-building and refurbishment faithful to the original plan. It now houses various speciality craft and retail enterprises.

▲ **Visit of the Prince of Wales to Brougham Hall, 1894.**

This photograph commemorates the visit to Brougham Hall, in September 1894, of Albert Edward, Prince of Wales, as the guest of Sir Henry Charles Brougham and his wife Zoe. On the far left stands Colonel Stanley Clarke, a member of the Royal Household, and on the far right Lord Brougham. Behind Lady Brougham (widow of Sir Richard Courtenay Musgrave), stands her son Sir Richard George Musgrave and, seated on the far right, his brother Philip Musgrave. The group was photographed on 18 September, the young Sir Richard Musgrave and his brother having come to lunch at Brougham Hall. The Prince afterwards went with them to the Musgrave family seat, Eden Hall, where they had tea.

B
A S
17.09

▷5   Working People

▲ **James Parkin - 'Jimmy the Bellman', c1900.**

James Parkin of Burrowgate (1846-1907), was the last of the Penrith 'bellman' or towncriers and the eighth whose name we know for certain, the earliest being Thomas Dawson who was appointed in 1811. In an age when newspapers were expensive and literacy was less prevalent their role was a significant one, being officially employed to deliver information and to announce meetings, sales, or notify the loss or finding of property. Following three slowly rung peals they would also convey news of deaths and 'bidden funerals', informing people from which house and at what time the procession would leave. They might have met up again later with Jimmy Parkin for he also 'blew' the organ in St Andrew's Church. In the latter half of the nineteenth century Saturdays and Tuesdays were the usual 'crying'days with notices being given around the Musgrave Monument, then repeated outside the Crown Hotel, the foot of Wordsworth Street, Sandgate, Castlegate and Great Dockray, where Jimmy is seen here, outside the Gloucester Arms Hotel. The bell they used has survived and can be seen at Penrith Museum.

▲ **John Davidson of Shepherd's Hill, Penrith, c1900.**

In 1874 Mr John Davidson purchased the property named Shepherd's Hill, off Stricklandgate, and lived there until his death in 1907. Writing in the PENRITH OBSERVER in September 1946, the editor remarked 'Mr Davidson was a noted Penrith character, a typical John Bull, still well remembered in the town. For many years he was manager of Penrith Auction Mart Company and he also farmed at Shepherd's Hill. He was quartermaster of the Yeomanry, and those who remember him say that he was an imposing figure on horseback.' After his day, Mr T E Altham bought the property.

▲ **John Davidson (extreme left) outside Shepherd's Hill, c1900.**

Shepherd's Hill recalls the name of its owners, the Shepherd family. In 1786 the site, then known as Shepherd's Croft, was sold to Thomas Clark of Watermillock, a partner in the nearby flourishing Old Brewery in Strickland-gate. In the 1860s and early 1870s the house became a school and among its pupils were J Simpson Yeates, Tom Altham and William Kirkbride, later prominent Penrithians.

▶ **Devonshire Street, Penrith, c1910.**

John, a nephew of John Davidson of Shepherd's Hill, stands in front of Arnison's shop in the centre of this photograph. At an early age he had been apprenticed to the clogger's business of Mr Robert Hunter and spent his life in this trade, acquiring a reputation as a skilled and conscientious workman. A member of the old Volunteers, Mr Davidson was for a long time the official target marker at the Troutbeck and Whinfell ranges and also at the Penrith Rifle Club. In the days when the street lamps were lit and extinguished by hand, he was one of the town's lamp lighters, and for some years was a member of the Penrith Fire Brigade. The tall building on the left in this photograph, where the rooftop aerials may be seen, was Penrith's first telephone exchange.

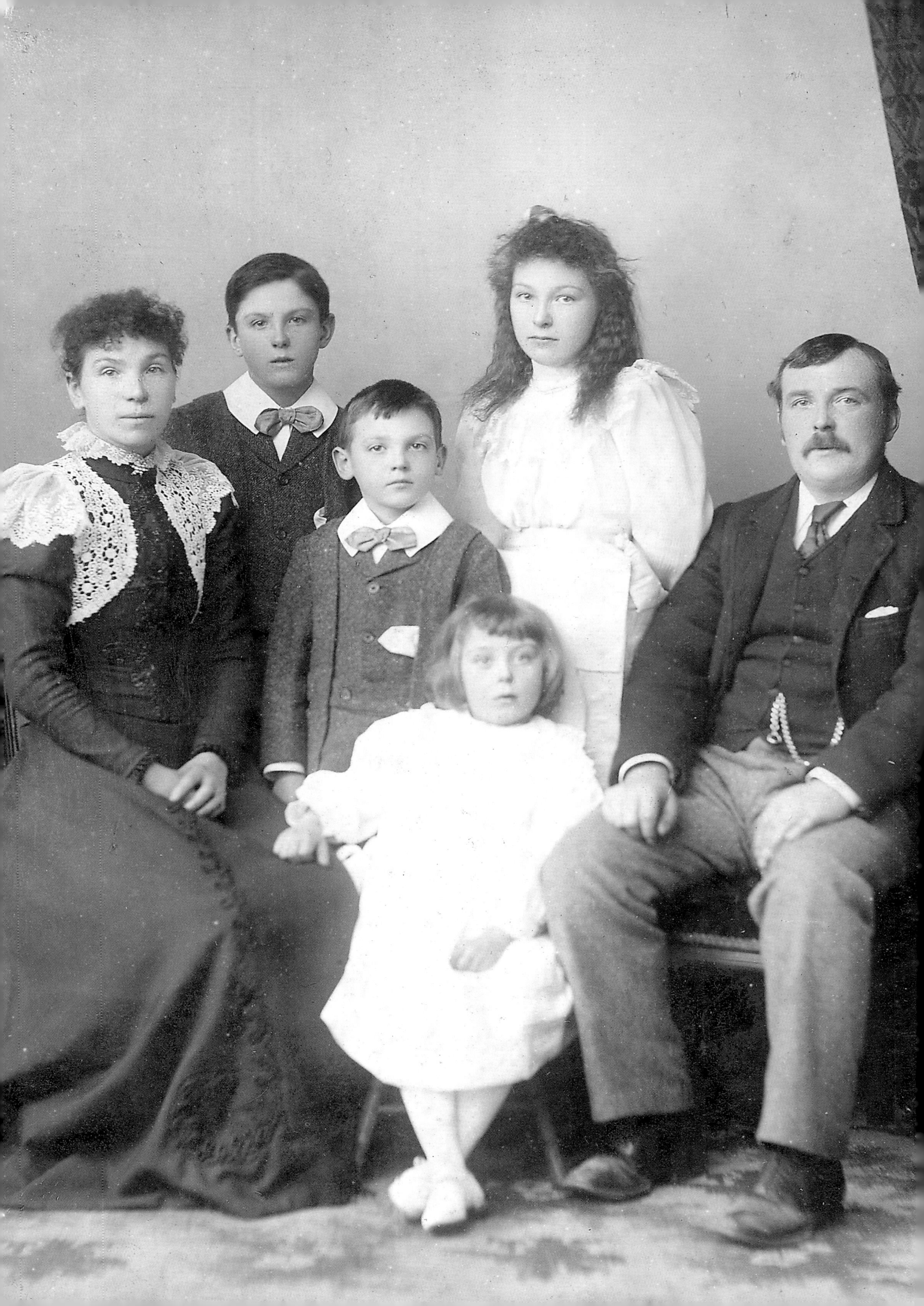

▲ **Edenhall Estate Workers, c1910.**

Wide-brimmed hats and a shotgun impart a frontier atmosphere in this group of workers on the Edenhall estate. The men and women in the front row are shod with clogs; the girl in contrast is smartly dressed and wearing soft leather boots.

◀ **George Davidson and family of Edenhall, c1897.**

George Davidson (seated right), worked as a carpenter and later as clerk of works on the Edenhall estate, walking from Penrith each day until he moved to Rose Cottage in the village in 1889. Married in 1885, his wife Barbara was the first treasurer of the Edenhall Women's Institute. From an album that belonged to the Davidson family we are shown glimpses of Edenhall village at work and play in the years preceding the First World War. As the photographs remind us, the estate employed a considerable number of servants, craftsmen and workers. They sustained a pattern of life which the Great War altered irrevocably.

▲ **Beating the carpets, Edenhall, c1910.**

Estate workers pause to be photographed while beating the carpets from the mansion at Eden Hall.

▲ Edenhall School, 1894.

▲ Celebrating the Coronation of King George V and Queen Mary in 1911.

▲ Edenhall village, c1900.

▼ **The Edenhall Shorthorn Sale, c1894.**

This sale took place on 10 August 1894, in the days when agriculture was the mainstay of the local economy. Men of the farming community attended the auction dressed in their best and exhibited all the decorum, sense of occasion and seriousness that might be expected at a religious gathering. Commercial in essence, these gatherings were also an outlet for social contact and conviviality.

R
W M
1717

D6 On the Move

46249

▲ Victoria Road, Penrith, c1910.

A farmer returns home down Victoria Road, his horse and cart laden with empty milk churns. At this time motor cars were seldom seen, and horses were still the mainstay of transport. Market days saw the streets of Penrith lined with horse-drawn vehicles of every description. There were 'digbies' - all-round tub-carts with the door at the back, beloved by farmers' wives for their warmth, and for what could be piled into them. There were high-seated 'dog carts' for those who had the better sorts of horses, and there were 'floats' for those who brought in a lot of produce. Stables were to be found everywhere, up every alleyway and in yards behind the licensed houses. They were filled to capacity on market days, often two horses to a stall. Over a hundred horses could be stabled under cover in the Crown Inn yard alone.

▲ **The Crown Inn, King Street, Penrith, c1885.**

The Crown was one of the town's busiest coaching inns and this scene shows the Ullswater coach about to leave with a full contingent of passengers. The photograph shows considerable evidence of retouching. The sky has been brushed in, tonal shading has been applied to the awning over the window of adjacent premises, to the figures leaving the inn and the horses awaiting them. The de-focussed area to the far right has also been scumbled in, probably by applying pigment with a dry brush. Although most often used in portraiture to make cosmetic improvements to a sitter's appearance, retouching could also be far more extensively employed to correct perceived defects in the print, for example to counter any blurring where there was movement.

▲ **The Ullswater coach at the Sun Hotel, Pooley Bridge, c1890.**
This service operated from Penrith railway station to Pooley Bridge ('for Lake Ullswater') twice daily.

▲ **SY Raven at Pooley Bridge pier, c1900.**

Raven was launched in 1889 and with her sister ship Lady of the Lake, built in 1877, provided cruises on Ullswater, running from Glenridding to Howtown and Pooley Bridge. Contructed of iron on the Clyde by Joseph Seath & Company of Rutherglen near Glasgow, Raven was transported in sections by rail to Penrith then by road to Pooley Bridge and assembled on the shores of Ullswater at Eller Beck from where she was launched. SY Raven had been commissioned by the Ullswater Navigation and Transit Company Limited largely in response to public pressure from visitors for trips on Ullswater. The company operated steamer services as early as 1855 carrying mail, provisions and passengers about the lake. The case for this sister boat to Lady of the Lake had been pressed by the travel agent Thomas Cook, who organised holidays to the Lakes from the south; he was concerned that should Lady of the Lake break down a second vessel would be available as back-up. After Raven was launched still more visitors poured in, often arriving in Penrith by train, then by horse-drawn charabanc to Pooley Bridge. While staying at Lowther Castle in 1912 as guest of Lord Lonsdale, the 'Yellow Earl', Kaiser Wilhelm II took a trip on Raven. All the deck work was painted yellow for that season.

▲ **Passengers outside Penrith railway station, 1906.**

The coming of the railways gave a dramatic boost to the growth of tourism, as did the introduction of paid holidays during the latter part of the nineteenth century. The Eden Valley Railway made it easier for workers in Northumberland, Durham and Yorkshire to see the beauties of the Lake District, while the Cockermouth, Keswick and Penrith line brought Keswick within seven hours of London. Here rail passengers board coaches destined for the Lakes. Horse-drawn wagonettes were owned by F Armstrong of The George Hotel, and T Siddle of The Crown, who also owned the Mosley pictured here. Though the railways had been seen as a major threat to horse-drawn coaches, it was the petrol engine which proved the real enemy.

▲ **Day-trippers off to Ullswater, c1908.**

The Penrith and District Motor Service angered the horse-drawn coach owners by introducing twenty-four seater motorised charabancs on the Ullswater tourist route in 1904. At first the gears were too light for the rough roads and many breakdowns occurred. AO545, a Durham Churchill with solid tyres and a top speed of 12 mph, was purchased by the company in 1907.

▲ **One of Ernie Hartness's motor coaches in Scotland Road, Penrith, 1946.**

Mr Ernest Hartness of Skelton Road Ends, near Penrith, developed his one man carrier's business from a pair of horses and a wagonette to a successful bus service with forty-three motor coaches and sixty employees. This photograph shows some of the passengers boarding one of the fifteen coaches setting off on the Townhead trip to Morecambe in 1946. The driver was Ernie's niece Miss Rose Robinson, with Anne Banks next to her in the passenger seat.

▶ **Tuer's Motors of Morland, 1939.**

Drivers Mr Joe Robinson (left) and Mr Dick Robinson (right) are here photographed in Morland village, resting against one of Tuer's Leyland Cub lorries.

▲ **Langwathby, c1910.**

In July 1903 there was great excitement in Penrith for the town was invaded by people who had gathered to see the first ever aeroplane fly over Cumberland and Westmorland as part of the Daily Mail Round Britain Air Race. Later, in July 1914, exhibition flights were given by a Monsieur Salmet whose monoplane, like a huge dragonfly, flew over the town. However this photograph of a monoplane over the village of Langwathby is a clever fake. The photographer was Mr Thomas Glaister, a monumental sculptor and resident of Langwathby until his death in 1915. A man with an inventive turn of mind, he carefully posed this group of village people, all looking towards the sky, and made a negative onto which he superimposed an aeroplane made from a picture postcard bought on a trip to Blackpool.

▼ **Penrith railway station looking south, 1900.**

When this picture was taken on 11 August 1900 Penrith station was a busy place served with frequent passenger and goods trains on the main line and services on the Eden Valley and Keswick lines. The newsagent's stand can be seen on the 'down' platform.

▲ **Waiting for the train at Penrith station, 1934.**

Photographed by Charles Fearnsides, boys from the Council School and girls from the Grammar School wait for the train to take them on a day trip to Barrow.

▲ 'Steaming' through Penrith, c1950.

After a stop at Penrith station, Pacific No 46249 - CITY OF SHEFFIELD, here photographed by Alec Fraser, heads north for Carlisle. A commercial and newspaper photographer, Alec Fraser worked for both the PENRITH OBSERVER and later the CUMBERLAND AND WESTMORLAND HERALD. He made a major contribution to the pictorial history of this part of Cumbria and retired in 1979 after a career spanning almost thirty years. A well-known character in the local community, he died in January 2000 at the age of eighty-six.

▲ **The M6 Motorway near Junction 40 on the outskirts of Penrith, 1999.**

(Photograph by Val Corbett).

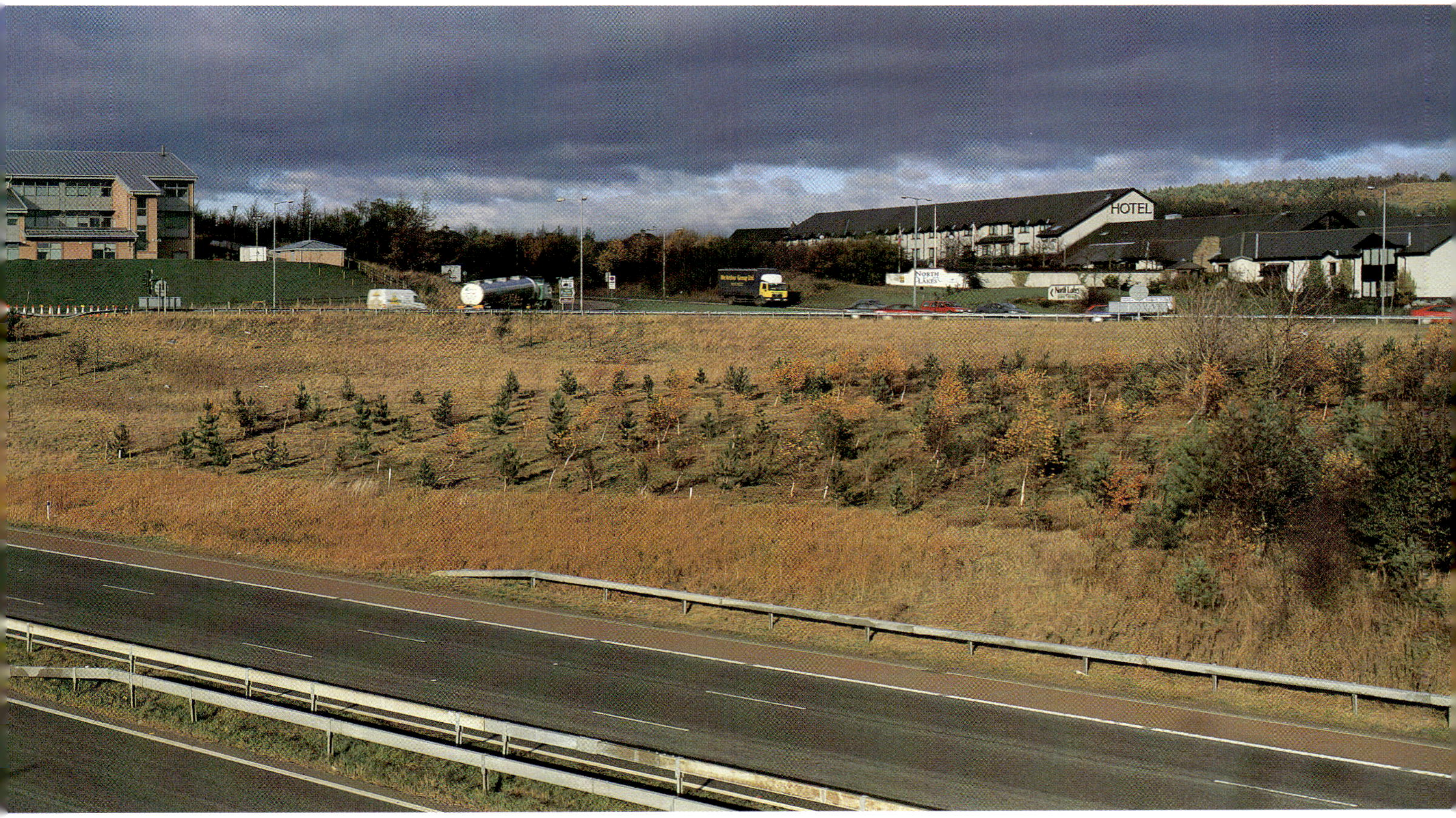
HOTEL

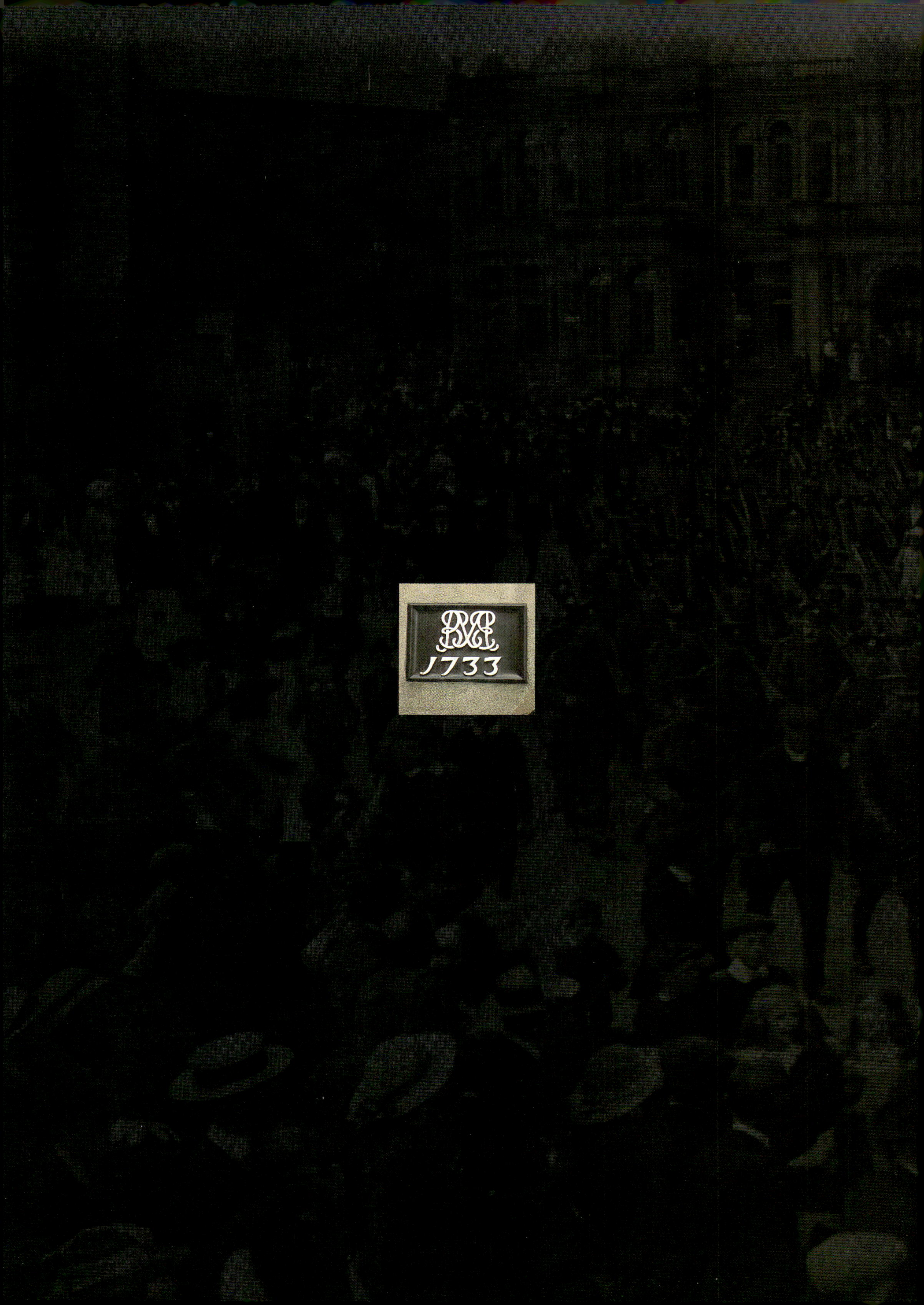
1733

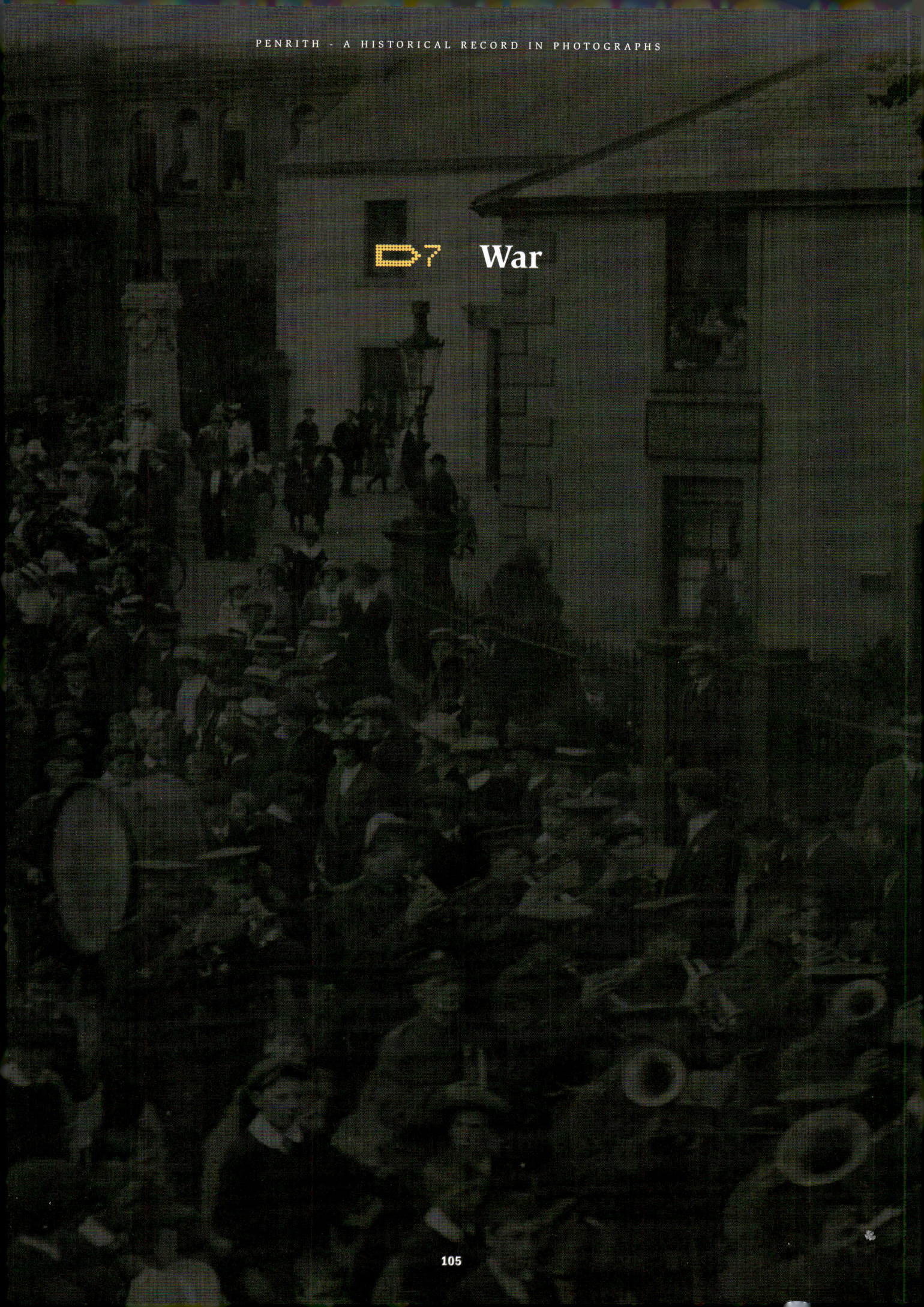

07 War

▲ **Officers of the Westmorland and Cumberland Yeomanry, c1865.**

Photographed by W Elliott, Photographic Artist, Penrith, in the front row appear - Major, the Hon Henry Lowther, later Third Earl of Lonsdale, (seated, third from left); Lieutenant Colonel Edward W Hassell, (seated, third from right); Adjutant Captain W Franklin (seated, far right). The origin of the Westmorland and Cumberland Yeomanry dates back to 1819 when the Yeomanry Cavalry Regiment was raised by Lieutenant Colonel Henry Cecil Lowther. He was followed as its first commander by Edward Hasell who remained its Colonel for fifty years. This militia superseded two earlier local volunteer forces, the Westmorland East and West Marches Local Militia and the Cumberland Loyal Leath Ward Volunteers. Its purpose was to support the civil powers during disturbances of the peace. It did so effectively in 1846 during the 'Navvy Riot' when law and order in and around Penrith hung in the balance as opposing factions of English and Irish labourers working on the Lancaster and Carlisle Railway converged on the town to settle their differences. Summer training camps were often held at Lowther in 'The Elysian Fields'. A company of the Yeomanry served as mounted infantry in the Boer War, and as Divisional Cavalry in the First World War seeing action at Gallipoli, as well as in France alongside three of Lord Kitchener's Army Divisions.

▲ **Officers of The 5th Cumberland (Inglewood) Rifle Volunteers, c1865.**

The Cumberland Rifle Volunteer Corps were raised in 1859, along with many others throughout the country, as a result of the menacing language of the French Emperor Napoleon III. The Penrith Corps was popularly known as the 'Inglewood Rifles'. Wednesday drills were held, according to the season, on the Fair Hill or in the Market Hall. They practised rifle shooting and engaged in mock combat in Lowther Park. Penrith Museum possesses an early example of a Lieutenant's uniform coat worn in the force. By comparing this photograph with another of the Inglewood Rifles dating from around the same time which was published in the PENRITH OBSERVER in 1930 it is evident that the figure seated in the centre of this group is Captain W B Arnison. When it appeared in the press the only members surviving were William Little of Hutton Hall (then aged ninety-seven), and retired tradesmen John Storey and John Sharp, cabinet makers, William Waterson, tobacconist, George Richardson, joiner, and George Irving, ironmonger.

▶ **Trooper William Pearson, Crimea War hero, in 1855.**

William Pearson (1826-1909) was born in King Street, Penrith, and was a leather dresser before he ran away to enlist in the 4th Light Dragoons in 1848. He was serving in Ireland when the regiment received orders for the Crimea. At Balaclava, during the 'Charge of the Light Brigade', he had an epaulette shot from his shoulder but survived the battle with a slight wound to his forehead. The severe Crimean winter left Pearson with frost-bite and he spent Christmas Eve 1854 having four toes amputated in the hospital at Scutari, where he was nursed by Florence Nightingale. Pearson received a Crimea Medal (with clasps for the battles at Alma, Balaclava, Inkerman and Sebastopol); he was also awarded the Turkish Medal and a Good Conduct Badge. This photograph was taken soon after his discharge on 16 March 1855. He was married six days later, having met his wife at a ball in honour of the Crimea heroes. Together they returned to Penrith, where Trooper Pearson became Inspecting Officer's Orderly for the Dalemain Troop of the Westmorland and Cumberland Imperial Yeomanry.

After discharge in 1855.

Left of Six Hundred.

▶ **William Pearson in 1894.**

In 1880 William Pearson moved to Underbarrow, near Kendal, where he set up a tanning business. He retired in 1906, and died on 31 July 1909, aged 82, and was buried with military honours in Parkside Cemetery in Kendal. This studio portrait was taken in 1894 by E Fowler Richards of Penrith to commemorate the 40th anniverary of the Charge. It was commissioned by Mr T D Graham who presented the original life-sized framed photograph to the people of Penrith. In 1971 a street in the town was named after Trooper Pearson (Pearson Court), and a plaque was erected at his birthplace. In 1978 Eden District Council purchased his set of medals and they can be seen, together with the photograph and other memorabilia, in Penrith Museum.

PRO PATRIA

IN MEMORY OF THE
MEN OF THIS TOWN AND
DISTRICT WHO FELL IN THE
SOUTH AFRICAN WAR
1899-1902.

▲ Survivors of the South African War, c1901.

Here we can see the members of the Penrith G and H Companies, 1st Volunteer Battalion, The Border Regiment, who fought in the Boer War in South Africa in 1890 and 1901. The photograph was taken shortly after the men returned from South Africa, and copies were presented to each of them by Mr James Scott, then chairman of the Penrith Urban District Council, for 'displaying true patriotism by giving up their civic and domestic station of life to loyally serve their Sovereign and Country through a most trying period of warfare'. In addition they were each presented with a gold watch on behalf of the Council, and Dr Haswell received a sword of honour. From left to right they are: rear, Privates Adam Irving, John Burrell, Thomas Davidson, John Boak, Robert Moffat, William Richardson and James Askins; middle, Lance-Corporal John Lawson, Private William Hindson (whose brother, John Hindson, was killed while serving with the Westmorland and Cumberland Yeomanry in South Africa), Sergeant James Smith, Lieutenant John Francis Haswell, Sergeant John Bell, Privates James Wilson, and James Sisson; front, Privates Joseph William Harrison, James Wright, Daniel Daly and Moses Dalton.

◀ The unveiling of the South African War Memorial in Penrith, 1906.

Familiarly known as the 'Black Angel', the unveiling took place in Corney Square on 1 March 1906, and was performed by Brigadier-General Michael F Rimington of Tynefield House who had achieved recognition in the campaign against the Boers as leader of the famous 'Rimington's Tigers'. The Penrith and District War Memorial Committee, having raised £346 by public subscription, issued invitations to tender for the memorial in November 1904. Eighteen competitors submitted designs, and eventually one of two designs by F W Doyle Jones of West Hartlepool and Chelsea was selected. The sculptor had already been chosen for memorials at Middlesborough, West Hartlepool and Gateshead, and the designs offered to Penrith were those adopted by the two latter places, which enabled the artist to undertake the memorial at less cost than a new design. The monument consists of a bronze figure, 'Peace Crowning the Heroes', standing on a pillar of Shap Granite, with an inscription 'PRO PATRIA - In memory of the men of this town and district who fell in the South African War, 1899-1902', and a list of the fallen. The Black Angel was moved to Castle Park in 1964 because it was felt that the fumes and pollution from traffic passing through the town were damaging the statue. In January 1999 a campaign was launched to have the monument returned to its original position in Corney Square.

▲ **Recruiting Staff for the First World War, c1914.**

This photograph, taken outside Penrith Town Hall, is inscribed on the reverse: 'Major G Varty Smith. Behind, T Hooson (formerly Regular Army) and J Booth (former Police Inspector). In front, Mrs Varty Smith and two daughters'.

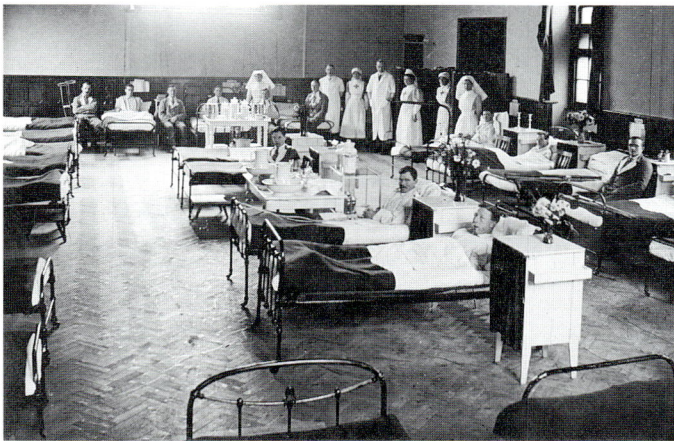

▲ **Soldiers leaving Penrith, 1914.**

Photographed by Charles Fearnsides, the Penrith Territorials marched along Middlegate to the railway station on 5 August 1914, and left for Barrow Barracks on the 5.00pm train.

▲ **Penrith Auxiliary Military Hospital, 1916.**

In February 1915 the wards at St Andrew's Parish Rooms, Skiddaw Grove and Wordsworth Hall were formed into one hospital by the War Office and were officially recognised as the Penrith Auxiliary Hospital, in the charge of Commandant Miss Thomson.

▲ **The War Memorial at the entrance to Castle Park, c1925.**

The fine stone gateway at the main entrance to the park, just opposite the railway station, is a memorial to the men and women from the town who gave their lives in the 1914-18 and 1939-45 Wars. Inside the gateway the names of the dead are inscribed on bronze panels.

▲ **Outside Penrith Town Hall on V E Day, 8 May 1945.**

Reverend Tom Cross, Congregational Minister, took these photographs showing the Town Hall decorated with flags and bunting (above), and a portion of the crowds in front of the Town Hall at 3.00 pm on V E Day (below).

▲ **Second World War evacuee David Morris and Kenneth Twentyman of Penrith, 1943.**

On the outbreak of war in September 1939 almost nine hundred pupils and staff of the Royal Grammar School in Newcastle upon Tyne were evacuated to Penrith. David Morris, who was then not quite thirteen, was billeted with Mr & Mrs William Twentyman in Newlands Terrace, remaining there until he left school in 1944. Photographed by William Tunley of Castlegate, David (left) is pictured in his ATC uniform alongside Mr & Mrs Twentyman's young son Ken, a member of the Army Cadet Force.

▲ **At the re-union in 1979.**

Ken Twentyman and David Morris (right) in July 1979 when the clock was turned back forty years as hundreds of 'evacuees' returned to Penrith for their first official re-union, eager to meet old friends and renew acquaintances. David Morris not only stayed in the same house in Newlands Terrace, but also slept in the same room. During his wartime residence like many evacuees he developed a great regard for the people of Penrith, and has kept in touch with his hostess's family all these years, although he now lives in Essex. The photograph was taken by Freddie Wilson for the CUMBERLAND AND WESTMORLAND HERALD.

▲ **Rememberance Day Parade, 1999.**

(Photographs by Val Corbett).

▷8 Shops and Inns

▲ **Henry Thompson, Furnishing and General Ironmonger, Market Square, c1900.**

A quality hardware shop, Henry Thompson's Ironmongers displays its wares the range and diversity of which is staggering by current standards. Thompson had acquired the business from Nesfield Robison in 1886 after working for Mr Robison for twenty-four years. In 1908 Henry Thompson moved to Castlegate and the property was subsequently demolished. The bank building now occupying this site was erected in 1912-13.

▲ **Middlegate, c1890.**

William Furness, printer and stationer, who had premises at No 3 Middlegate, published his HISTORY OF PENRITH in 1894 under the name 'Ewanian'. Also at No 3 were Maria and Elizabeth Jackson, dressmakers and milliners, while above them was the Working Men's Temperance Club. By the side of No 3 were saddlers Rennie and Wilkinson and at No 4 McVitties shoe shop, and George Lowthian, boot and shoe maker. Next door was William P Wilkinson, butcher, then draper Thomas Bell Todd. William Kirkbride had his chemist and druggist store at No 8, and at No 11 was James G Hill, grocer and provision dealer.

▲ **Ernest Dawson's grocers shop, Hunter Lane, c1930.**

Charles Fearnsides' photograph shows Mr Dawson and his son David behind the counter of their shop at the corner of Hunter Lane surrounded by hams, sausages and tins of biscuits.

▲ **Penrith Co-operative Society Boots and Shoes Department, Burrowgate, c1930.**

The three ladies standing inside the doorway are (left to right) Mrs Stout, Miss A A Turner and Miss E Pattinson.

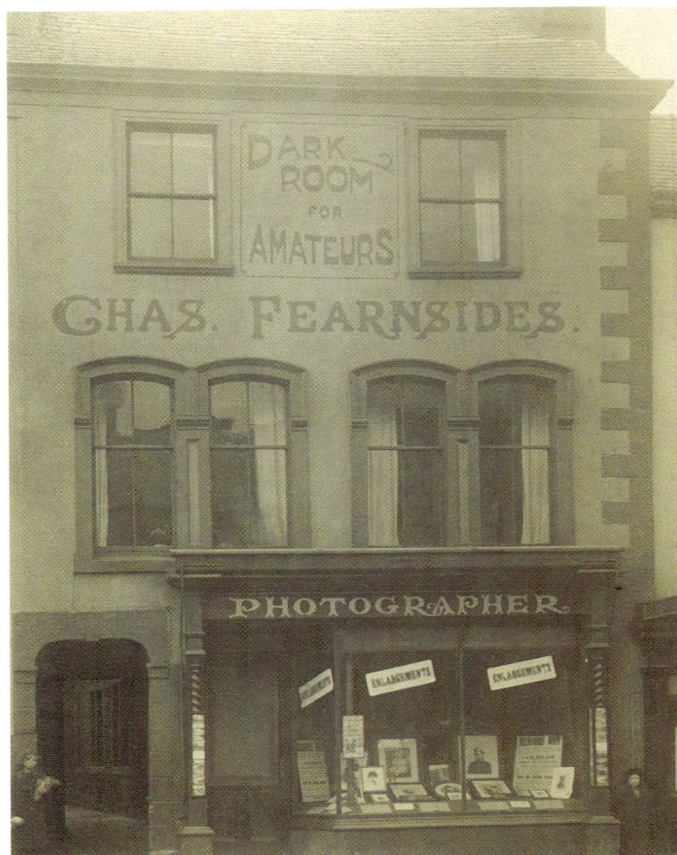

▲ **(Left) Penrith photographer Charles Fearnsides in his shop in Little Dockray.**

Charles Fearnsides (1882-1968) a native of Herefordshire, moved to Penrith in 1905. In 1908 he took over the business of photographer Fowler Richards in Victoria Road, embarking on a professional career which would last until his retirement in 1949. His reputation was enhanced considerably through an early opportunity to photograph the visit of King Edward VII to Brougham Hall. He was keen to encourage amateur photography making a room above his later premises in King Street available as a dark room for hire. During the First World War he was a Signaller in the Royal Garrison Artillery and during service in France used his camera skills to record bombed and war-ravaged scenes near Ypres and Courtrai. He was active in the community being a member of the Voluntary Auxiliary Defence and through his efforts Penrith Cottage Hospital acquired its first X-Ray equipment.

▲ **(Right) Fearnsides' earlier shop and studio in King Street.**

▲ **The Blue Bell Inn, Little Dockray, c1901.**

When this photograph was taken, the inn keeper was William Parkin. Later, in June 1914, Mr and Mrs Whitfield Pounder took over the tenancy and remained there until June 1926 when they retired and were succeeded by their son Thomas Pounder. The Blue Bell had its own 'eating house', which was famous for its weekly market day dinners. It was largely patronised by farmers and in the winter months a special meal of lentil soup with boiled beef and peas pudding was in great demand.

▲ The Gloucester Arms Hotel, Great Dockray, c1948.

Also known as Dockray Hall, a plaque on the front of the building says that it was 'traditionally the residence of Richard, Duke of Gloucester, afterwards Richard III', though there is no firm evidence for this. The Duke's arms of two boars rampant are prominently displayed above the main entrance. Over another doorway is the inscription 'IW 1580', the initials of John Whelpdale who remodelled the house. Writing of Penrith Castle in 1787, James Clarke tells us that 'an arched subterraneous road leads all the way from the castle to the kitchen-floor of a house in the town, called Dockray Hall', though the existence of the tunnel has never been proved.

▶ The Two Lions Hotel, Great Dockray, c1961.

Now set back behind a courtyard off Great Dockray, Colin Denwood's photograph shows that the entrance to the Two Lions Hotel used to be through a narrow alleyway next to the shop then occupied by Mr and Mrs Allison. The property was formerly the town house of Gerard Lowther, a forebear of the Earls of Lonsdale. Though much altered, the present structure dates from 1585, but parts of an older building may be incorporated in it. Particularly interesting is the plasterwork ceiling in what was the dining room. The White Horse Inn, seen on the right of the photograph, has a much shorter history, being first mentioned in 1834.

▶ Interior of the Two Lions Hotel, c1951.

This photograph, taken when the hotel was under the ownership of Mr Warren Bruce, shows the fireplace which bears the date 1585.

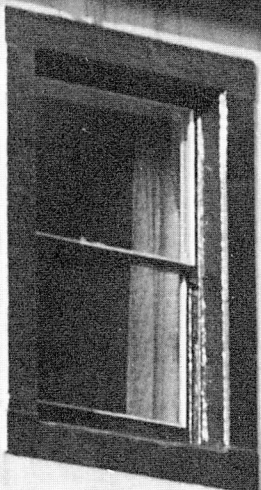

▲ **The Fish Hotel, Castlegate, c1961.**

The Fish Hotel stood on this site for many years, being mentioned in 1790. It was demolished in 1972 to make way for a new shopping precinct.

▲ **The entrance to Poet's Walk shopping precinct, 1984.**

◀ **The Robin Hood Inn, King Street, c1951.**

This building in King street is one of several sites in Penrith with rich literary associations. It was here, in October 1794, that the poet William Wordsworth nursed his friend Raisley Calvert who took ill as they were setting out on a vacation which would have taken them to Portugal: 'I have been here (Mr.Somerby's, at the sign of the Robin Hood, Penrith) for some time. I am still much worried with my sick friend; and sorry am I to add that he worsens daily ... he is barely alive'. After Calvert's death in January of the following year Wordsworth learned that he had been left £900 in his will. This provided him with the economic security needed to devote himself to his poetry rather than a professional career such as his family expected. They were of much the same station in life, Wordsworth being the son of an agent employed by Lord Lonsdale, while Calvert's father was a steward of the Duke of Norfolk at Greystoke near Penrith. In 1791 Raisley had inherited several farms deriving income which permitted him to pursue his interests in sculpture. He could thus sympathise with Wordsworth's ambitions and, through this final but far-sighted act of generosity, fostered their success.

▲ **The Royal Hussar Hotel, King Street, c1969.**

This hostelry was opened in 1794 as the New Crown Inn, so called as there was already a Crown Inn in King Street and the two co-existed right through the nineteenth century. The original inn became known as the Old Crown and when it closed in the early years of the twentieth century, the New Crown became the Crown, then the Royal Hussar. It was demolished some years ago and a supermarket was built on the site.

▶ **Glasson's Penrith Breweries, Cornmarket, c1950.**

In the mid-seventeenth century this building was referred to in the deeds as the 'Gambling Corner House' because a tailor of that name had his shop on this corner of Cornmarket and Great Dockray. It became a wine and spirits business, run by George Bird, before Glasson's Penrith Breweries bought the property in about 1900. The bar attached to their wine and spirits shop was called 'The Snug', also known as the 'Elbow Room', eventually becoming the Board and Elbow of today. The building to the left bears the date 1624 and was formerly the old Black Lion, though it was later incorporated into the Board and Elbow. The photographer of this wintry scene was Charles Fearnsides.

GLASSONS
PENRITH BREWERIES
WINE & SPIRIT MERCHANTS

▲ **Her Majesty the Queen and the Duke of Edinburgh at Penrith's Mansion House, May 1991.**
Photographer Freddie Wilson has captured the Queen's delight as she is presented with a box of Penrith toffee by Eden District Council's Chairman, Councillor Mac Carlyle.

▲ **The Toffee Shop, Brunswick Road, 1999.**
(Photograph by Val Corbett).

▶ **Arnison's Shop Front, 1999.**
(Photograph by Val Corbett).

R + L
Wharton
1781
annus in Diem
sed Nox venit

▷9 Sports and Pastimes

▲ **Penrith Sons of Temperance Band, c1900.**

The Oak Division of the Sons of Temperance was formed in 1880 and made such headway that in 1894 it decided to have a brass band of its own. In 1899 Mr Joseph Varty became bandmaster, an office which he held with distinction for twenty-one years. The members of the band pictured here are: front row - W Barker, Tom Bolt, C Wannop, [unknown], Joseph Sanderson; second row - Robert Gardiner, James Swainson, John Bamber, Fred Hodgson, Joseph Varty (bandmaster), William Johnston, H Thompson, J W Wilson; third row - W Grisenthwaite, James Grisenthwaite, N Dixon, W Pattinson, G Nichol, W Atkinson, T Sinkinson; back row - J Varty, S Thwaites, Hilton Watson, C H Varty, Sam Main, Aaron Wilson.

◄ **Inglewood Wanderers, c1897.**

The names of the gentlemen in this photograph are inscribed on the reverse. They are: back row standing - William Pattinson, William Wright, Tom Bolt(?), Elijah Pattinson, Tommy Mounsey, James Dargue, [unknown], George Bowman (Secretary); middle row - Herbert Hopes(?), Moses Wilson, George Reay, Andrew Borrowdale, Porky Pearson; front row - Jackie Woodhall, Walter Wilkinson, Tom Frankland.

Penrith Friars com. Diamond Jubilee 1930

▲ **The Subcription (Crown Square) Bowling Club.**

The Subscription Club was attached to the Conservative Club and had its green near the Two Lions Hotel.

▲ **Penrith Friar's Bowling Club Diamond Jubilee Committee, 1930.**

▲ **Carriage driver George Bowman Junior at the Lowther Horse Driving Trails.**
(Photograph by Freddie Wilson).

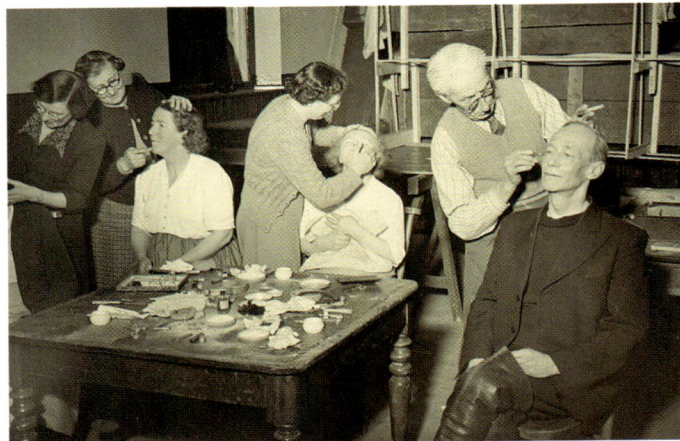

▲ **The team of 'Gardeners Question Time' in Penrith Town Hall, 1953.**

Fred Loads, Freddie Grisewood, Alan Gemmell and Bill Sowerbutts were photographed by Eric Davidson on 7 November 1953, when the programme was broadcast live from the Town Hall by the BBC.

▲ **Penrith Playhouse, Castlegate, c1950.**

Charles Fearnsides, pictured second from the right, was a founder member of the Penrith Players. He produced over thirty plays as well as serving as make-up artist and was regarded as a fine character actor. He appeared in Liddy, the play which took the society to third place in the British Drama League in 1935 and produced the one-act play Father Cyprian to mark the society's Silver Jubilee.

▲ **The cast of the Penrith Pageant in Castle Park, 1951.**

Staged by the Penrith Players to celebrate the Festival of Britain, members of the cast of the Pageant were photographed by Eric Davidson, Portrait and Commercial Photographer of Thackagate, Penrith.

◀ **Freddie Wilson of Penrith winning the pole vault at Penrith Gala, c1955.**

Regarded as one of Cumbria's premier athletic events, Penrith Gala flourished in two eras of time, separated by almost forty years. The original gala, which took place on the Foundry field, was introduced during the 1800s, by the town's friendly societies, the Oddfellows, Druids and Foresters. Following a financial crisis in 1911 the event fell into abeyance. It was revived in 1949 on the Football (or Kilgour's) field, under the presidency of Viscount Lowther. This photograph was taken by Frank Boyd, retired postman and amateur photographer of Castlegate, Penrith, whose book, AROUND PENRITH IN OLD PHOTOGRAPHS, has played an important part in fostering interest in historic images of the town and district.

▼ **Penrith Rugby Union Football Club, 1999.**

(Photograph by Val Corbett).

▷10   The Changing Face

▲ **Wordsworth House, c1890.**

Built in 1792 as two houses in the style of Robert Adam, that on the left came into the possession of the poet Wordsworth's first cousins John and Richard in 1805. John, who resided there, captained the 'Earl of Abergavenny', a position in which he was followed by his namesake the poet's brother. The writer Thomas De Quincey stayed here on a brief visit in 1807. A letter of Dorothy Wordsworth dated 23 December 1815 seems to suggest that she was a guest here for about three nights, the last of which saw her brother William arrive with other members of the family for dinner. He stayed until the following morning when he walked with Dorothy to Lowther and then to Sockbridge.

▲ **Construction work on Wordsworth House for the new Penrith Town Hall, 1906.**

The two eighteenth century houses were converted in 1905-6 to create Penrith Town Hall, a development which provoked lively debate, critics holding that the architectural integrity and appeal of the building would be lost. Co-founder of the National Trust, Canon Rawnsley, pleaded successfully for the retention of several features, including some windows and the central staircase. The new design was the work of J J Knewstubb, the Council's Surveyor and Engineer, and the main contractor was Joseph McDonald of Graham Street, Penrith. He can be seen in this photograph standing on the porch above the entrance door, wearing a light-coloured hat. The photograph was taken by Edward McDonald, a relation of Joseph, who had a photographic studio, first in Angel Lane and then at 48, Castlegate. A section of the ground floor on the north side of the Town Hall served as the Public Library until 1992. For many years the town's Museum also had its home there; it is now located in Robinson's School where many of the original artefacts are stored and displayed.

▲ **Penrith Market Day, c1911.**

The building beyond the Musgrave Monument, which at that time housed the Bank of Liverpool and Bowerbank's Ironmongers, was demolished in 1912.

▲ **Looking across to St Andrew's Church soon after the demolition.**

The new bank, which was built on the site, opened in July 1913.

▲ **Meeting House Lane, 1958.**

Seven cottages in Meeting House Lane, including Mrs Jessie Campbell's sweet shop, were demolished in April 1958 under the Urban Council's slum clearance programme. The old road was re-aligned and widened across the top of Sandgate, and two new bungalows for elderly people replaced the cottages.

▼ Duke Street, 1957.

Penrith photographer Alec Fraser recorded the demolition of condemned housing at the junction of Duke Street and Stricklandgate in February 1957. The three-storeyed block comprised nine sub-standard houses, six in Duke Street and three in Wilson Row. It had been declared a clearance area in 1935, but demolition was delayed because of the war.

▶ Scaws housing estate, 1949.

Photographed by J L Topaz soon after completion in 1949, these stone-fronted houses at the foot of Scaws estate took pride of place for imaginative planning and visual appeal in the post-war housing development of Penrith. Designed by architect Frank Blanc, with Bob Reay as the main contractor, the new estate was described by the local press as 'Penrith's garden city', but costs and government restrictions meant that later houses could not be built to such high standards.

▶ Brentfield Way on Scaws estate, 1949.

▲ **Market Square and Devonshire Street, c1880.**

A summer's morning finds Penrith enjoying an almost eerie tranquillity in this view taken around 1880, looking north from a cobbled Market Place into Devonshire Street. By the mid-nineteenth century the town's more important commercial and domestic buildings, built largely of red sandstone, bore the stamp of Georgian and Regency classical-style architecture. The building in buff stone of the gothic Musgrave Monument in 1861 could not have provided a greater contrast. Isolated aesthetically as well as physically, the Monument serves, nevertheless, as a visual link in the north-south axis of the town from Middlegate to King Street.

▲ **The Musgrave Monument and Devonshire Street, January 2000.**

The Musgrave Monument has become perhaps the town's most distinctive feature - to many it is emblematic of Penrith. It was not surprising therefore that the suggestion in 1999 to re-site the monument by moving it a short distance as part of the town centre enhancement scheme met with strong criticism. Penrithians and visitors alike will continue to discuss at length the faults and merits of the scheme, which included the laying of granite sets, new 'herringbone' parking bays, the introduction of pelican-type crossing and the erection of gas-lamp style lighting. (Photograph by Val Corbett).

▲ **Angel Square.**

(Photograph by Barry Stacey).

▼ **Environment Agency North Area Office, 1999.**

(Photograph by Val Corbett).

▲ **Oasis Holiday Village.**

(Photograph by Val Corbett).

Acknowledgements

Grateful thanks are extended to the following for commenting on the text for this book: Robert Bartle, Gordon Browne, Ian Bruce, David Clarke, Ron Dearden, Jeremy Godwin, Steve Huddart, John Hurst, Denis Perriam and Mrs Pauline Robinson. Ron Dearden kindly supplied information about some of Penrith's earliest photographers. For supplying details for some of the captions: Mrs Eleanor Beattie, Peter Connon, Frances Dimond (Royal Archives, Windsor), Stuart Eastwood (Border Regiment and King's Own Royal Border Regiment Museum, Carlisle), the late Jim Monkhouse, Tim Padley (Tullie House Museum, Carlisle), Ernest Robinson and Kenneth Twentyman. The Cumberland & Westmorland Herald (Colin Maughan), Frank Boyd, Lawrence Marlow and Mrs Helen Sourbut kindly permitted the reproduction of photographs in their ownership. Thanks are also extended to photographers Val Corbett, Barry Stacey and Freddie Wilson for their cooperation and support, and to Dennis George for compiling the index. The production of a book of this nature would not have been possible without the generous gifts of photographs to the collections of Penrith Museum over many years. Eden District Council gratefully acknowledges these donors.

Sources and Further Reading

Allison, J - *Picturesque Pocket Companion: Comprising a Succinct Descriptive Sketch of Penrith etc ...* - (Penrith,1836)
Arthurton, R S & Wadge, A J - *Geology of the Country around Penrith* - (London 1981)
Baldwin, G - *Looking at Photographs: A Guide to Technical Terms* - (London, 1991)
Baldwin, J R, & Whyte, A D (eds) - *The Scandinavians in Cumbria* - (Edinburgh, 1985)
Boyd, F - *Around Penrith in Old Photographs* - (Stroud, 1993)
Clarke, J - *A Survey of the Lakes of Cumberland, Westmorland and Lancashire* - (London, 1787)
Collingwood, W G - *The Giant's Grave, Penrith* - (Cumberland and Westmorland Antiquarian and Archaeological Society Transactions, 1922)
Corbett, V - *A Rhythm, a Rite and a Ceremony: Helen Sutherland at Cockley Moor 1939-1965* - (Penrith, 1996)
Fell, C I - *Early Settlement in the Lake Counties* - (London, 1972)
Furness, W - [pseudonym: 'Ewanian'], *History of Penrith* - (Penrith, 1894)
Higham, N - *The Northern Counties to AD 1000* - (Harlow, 1986)
Horsley, J E - *Jottings about Old-time Penrith* - (Penrith, 1926)
Hutchinson, W - *History of Cumberland* - (Carlisle, 1794) Reprint 1974
Jefferson, S - *History and Antiquities of Leath Ward in the County of Cumberland* - (Carlisle, 1840)
Lambert, J, Newman, R and Olivier, A (eds) - *Transect Through Time: The Archaeological Landscape of the Shell North Western Ethylene Pipeline* - (Lancaster, 1996)
Lindop, G - *A Literary Guide to the Lake District* - (London, 1993)
Mains, B & Tuck, A (eds) - *Royal Grammar School, Newcastle upon Tyne* - (London, 1986)
Owen, H - *The Lowther Family* - (Chichester, 1990)
Pallister, G - *Evacuation* - (Newcastle upon Tyne, 1979)
Perriam, D R - *Penrith Castle* - (unpublished article)
Perriam, D R & Robinson, J - *The Medieval Fortified Buildings of Cumbria* - (Cumberland and Westmorland Antiquarian and Archaeological Society Extra Series 29, 1998)
Pevsner, N - *The Buildings of England: Cumberland and Westmorland* - (Harmondsworth 1967)
Robertson, D & Koronka, P - *Secrets and Legends of Old Westmorland* - (Kirkby Stephen, 1992)
Rollinson, W (ed) - *The Lake District: Landscape Heritage* - (Newton Abbot, 1989)
Sandford, E - *A Cursory Relation of all the Antiquities and Familyes in Cumberland, circa 1675* - (Cumberland and Westmorland Antiquarian and Archaeological Society Tract Series 4, 1890)
Scott, D - *History of Penrith Church* - (Penrith, 1922)
Shotter, D - *Romans and Britons in North West England* - (Lancaster, 1993)
Sim, I G - *Under the Shadow of the Beacon: A Few Penrith and District Memories of the Years 1939-1945* - (Penrith, 1945)
Stretton, E H A - *Dacre Castle* - (Penrith, 1994)
Thomas, M - *A History of Brougham Hall & Highhead Castle* - (Chichester, 1992)
Walker, J - *History of Penrith* - (Penrith, 1858)
Winchester, A J L - *Landscape and Society in Medieval Cumbria* - (Edinburgh, 1987)

Index